Emotional I

Practical Guide

How to Retrain Your Brain to Win Friends, Influence People, Improve your Social Skills, Achieve Happier Relationships, and Raise Your EQ

Table of Contents

Introduction 7

Part I: 11

What You Need to Know About Emotional
Intelligence 11

Chapter 1: Emotional Intelligence Essential
Facts 13

Understanding Emotions 14

Understanding Empathy 22

Understanding Temperament 27

Chapter 2: Emotional Intelligence 33

Defining Emotional Intelligence 35

Importance of Emotional Intelligence.............. 37

Applications of Emotional Intelligence............. 40

Chapter 3: The Emotional Intelligence
Framework 53

Breaking down Emotional Intelligence..............54

Self-Awareness 58

Self-Management...63

Social Awareness 67

Relationship Management 70

Interrelationship of Emotional Intelligence
Components. 74

Part II: 77

Chapter 4: What is an Emotional Intelligence Test? 79

How EQ Is Tested 83

Why Test for EQ? 86

What to Expect in an EQ Test 89

Sample Questions and Answers 92

Chapter 5: Measuring Emotional Intelligence 99

How Emotional Intelligence Is Measured 100

How to Use Your Emotional Quotient to
Understand Your Needs..................................... 103

The Emotional Intelligence Scale..................... 106

Chapter 6: Emotional Intelligence Self-Assessment 119

Instructions for this Assessment 120

Self-Awareness... 122

Self-Management 127

Social Awareness.. 132

Relationship Management................................. 137

Calculating Your Scores................................... 143

Your Results 145

Part III: 155

Practical Tips to Improve Emotional Intelligence 155

Chapter 7: 50 Practical Tips to Improve Self-Awareness 157

Chapter 8: 50 Practical Tips to Improve Self-Management 175

Chapter 9: 50 Practical Tips to Improve Social Awareness 193

Chapter 10: 50 Practical Tips to Improve Relationship Management 211

Conclusion 227

Introduction

Have you ever had a time where you reacted poorly in an emotionally charged situation, and your reaction resulted in a situation that you wish was different? Perhaps you have had a bad day at work, and when you got home, you lashed out at your spouse and children out of frustration when they played a game just a bit too loudly for your taste.

Though they were having a blast playing together, they annoyed you, and you said things you regret. As a result, your children went to bed upset with you after calling you a meanie-head and saying they wished you were still at work, and you angered your spouse, who chose to sleep on the couch instead of in bed with you. After your outburst, you are left with the guilt weighing on your conscience, a wish to change on your mind, and the assumption that the kind of change you would like to see is an impossibility in your heart. You may feel as though you are not the person your family deserves due to your inability to deal with emotional situations.

The reason you reacted so poorly to the situation is due to a low level of emotional intelligence. Emotional intelligence is believed to be one of the most accurate predictors of success and happiness in life, and those who are lacking average or high levels of emotional intelligence often find themselves struggling socially, especially when emotions are running high. We all have natural levels of emotional intelligence, influenced by upbringing and general temperament, much like how we have natural levels of intelligence, but unlike intelligence, emotional intelligence levels are flexible.

You can build your emotional intelligence and influence your ability to read and react to emotional situations. This means that you can improve your EQ (emotional quotient; the measurement of your emotional intelligence), and improve your social skills and relationships, though it will take effort.

Imagine if you had a higher EQ in the above situation: You would have come home from work angry, but instead of lashing out at your family, you took a deep breath, recognized that your family was having fun, and went to take a quiet drive around town for fifteen minutes to yourself to unwind before returning home and joining in on playtime and your children's bedtime routines. Instead of them being upset and angry at you, your children told you they love you, told you that you are the best, and went to bed happily. You then were able to spend time with your spouse, calmly explaining the situation and why you were angry, which gained you the emotional support of your spouse as well. Ultimately, you were able to handle the situation tactfully, and despite the anger you felt, you bettered your relationships with your spouse and children.

With the help of this book, you will be provided the skills you will need to bolster your EQ and develop the ability to handle social situations with tact. You will be guided through the basics of EQ, provided tests to see where your current EQ levels are, and then given plenty of tips to improve on your EQ levels. You are not destined to remain at low levels of EQ forever; putting in the effort to boost your skills is entirely possible, and you can achieve the high EQ you and those around you deserve.

Part I:
What You Need to Know
About Emotional Intelligence

Chapter 1: Emotional Intelligence Essential Facts

Before delving into what emotional intelligence is and how it works, you must first learn to understand the concepts that underlie it. Every person feels emotions and has a unique temperament, and most people experience empathy in some capacity. These combine and create your reactions to emotionally volatile situations. Each of these relates intricately with emotional intelligence and having an understanding of what causes these and why we have them is a key to raising it. By knowing how these relate to emotional intelligence, you can work with them as opposed to against them, seeing much quicker progress than going in blindly. Those with low EQ are typically slaves to their temperaments and emotions and react as such, whereas those who have a high EQ are typically much more empathetic and in control over both themselves and their situations.

Understanding Emotions

There are several human emotions, all composed of basic emotions that can combine into a wide spectrum of what is felt from day to day. It is believed that emotions can be reduced down to four basic feelings: happiness, sadness, anger, and fear. Every emotion you may feel, from surprise to guilt or disgust, are all subsets of those four emotions. These four are believed to be biologically ingrained into us through evolution, though it is possible to develop more nuanced or complicated feelings through sociological sources, such as cultural influence.

The Purpose of Emotions

These four emotions must be important if they have evolved over time to be universal: Almost any human from any culture can see a picture of another human making any of those four expressions and know exactly what it is. The reason for this is to be able to quickly and clearly communicate with other humans. By developing both expressions of universal emotions, humans pave the way to develop empathy as well.

Each of the four universal emotions conveys something different: They identify different situations and needs. Happiness conveys that all needs are being met. Sadness conveys that something bad has happened or something or someone important has been lost or harmed and indicates that there is a need for support to encourage healing. Anger conveys the sense of being wronged, whether being taken advantage of or getting betrayed, and it indicates a need for boundaries or protection. Fear conveys that there is a threat or danger nearby and that there is a need for safety.

As a social species, we need to be able to communicate our basic needs in order to ensure everyone's needs are met. If we do not know how our neighbors are doing, we never know whether they need extra help or support, or if we are angering them and need to take a step back. Through communication, everyone's needs are met more efficiently, and the easiest way to communicate those needs is through universal body language. With body language and emotions, we can see, at a glance, how those around us are feeling. We can also tell the intentions of strangers by being able to see signs of anger on their expressions, or if they are happy, scared, or sad. Communicating at a glance without needing to observe and process words or more convoluted forms of communication allows for quick snap-judgments to be made, enabling for quicker reactions as well.

Emotions also have internal connotations as well. These can encourage or motivate us to act in certain ways, as well as help general survival. If you feel afraid, your body prepares to flee or fight in order to keep you alive. If you are angry, your body prepares to protect itself. Happiness causes relaxation and encourages you to engage in more of the behaviors that triggered the happiness, to begin with, and sadness encourages us to protect those we love or change our situations to something that brings us joy.

The Cause of Emotions

There are several different theories on what causes emotions, but the three most common are the James-Lange theory, the Cannon-Bard theory, and the Schacter-Singer model. Each of these is slightly different and offer various explanations.

The James-Lange Theory believes that emotion is a person's understanding of the physiological changes the body creates in response to a stimulus. If a person sees a snake and feels his extremities begin to tingle, his heart race, and his breathing quicken as he hyper-focuses on the snake in front of him, he knows that what he is physically feeling is fear and responds in that manner. In this theory, the physical changes come first, and the mind labels the physical changes as the emotion in order to understand them.

The Cannon-Bard theory believes that we sense things around us with our five senses, and the information sensed is sent through the nervous system to the brain, where two different parts receive the message. The cortex, or the front of the brain, receives one message and responds to the message while the hypothalamus receives a second copy of the message and creates the physical reactions. In this case, the man sees the snake. His eyes send the message that he has seen a snake to both his cortex and hypothalamus.

The cortex creates the emotion in response to the stimulus while the hypothalamus creates the physical response. The physical and emotional responses combine together to create the emotion of fear.

The Schacter-Singer model believes that fear is a combination of physical responses to a stimulus paired with conscious thoughts on the stimulus. The two of these together create a general feeling toward the stimulus, which is interpreted as the emotion. For example, the man who has seen a snake may feel his heartbeat quicken in response to the snake, but his feeling depends on his cognitive thoughts on the idea of snakes. If he believes that snakes are quite fascinating and loves to look at them, that heartbeat quickening may be interpreted as happiness, but if he has learned that snakes are dangerous and should be avoided at all costs, that same increase in pulse combined with those beliefs would create a feeling of fear.

James-Lange Theory	Emotion is the person's interpretation of physical changes to the body in response to a stimulus
Cannon-Bard Theory	The body sends information from the senses to the cortex, which creates emotion, and hypothalamus of the brain, which creates physical responses such as crying or shaking in fear
Schacter-Singer Model	Emotion is created when physical changes and conscious thoughts over a stimulus combine

Conflict of Rationality vs. Emotionality

Oftentimes, in our minds, we are constantly hovering somewhere between rational and emotional. The emotional part of our minds was born first, designed to keep us alive long enough to reproduce. The rational part of our minds is what makes us distinctly human: It allows us the ability to act in ways that are contradictory to our emotions in order to get a better result. We allow emotions to influence our thoughts and decisions, but allow the rational part of our minds to police the emotional part to keep it in balance. In order to be successful people, especially in workplaces and relationships, we need a healthy balance between both rationality and emotionality. Sometimes, however, we find our sense of rationality drowned out by the emotional side of our minds. In this instance, the person would be entirely enslaved to the emotions. Consider that the person afraid of snakes has a snake phobia, and upon seeing a harmless garden snake slither in front of him, goes into a panic attack and freezes at the sight. In this case, he was ruled by his emotions; his rational side of his brain, which would have reminded him that the snake is tiny and harmless, was silenced by the emotion of fear.

The Relevance of Emotions to Emotional Intelligence

This battle of rationality and emotionality relates directly to emotional intelligence: It is the ability to identify those emotions, manage them, and balance them in such a way that allows for rational thinking. A high EQ means that you are likely to be adept at managing your emotions and giving them the consideration they deserve while still keeping them in check and allowing rationality to rule. This allows for levelheadedness, which allows the man afraid of snakes to simply walk away mildly perturbed at having seen a snake, but still fully capable of functioning.

Understanding Empathy

Empathy is the ability to understand and feel another person's feelings as if you, yourself, were experiencing them. Empathy allows you to take one look at a grieving widow and feel her pain strongly enough to motivate you to help her, or that allows you to feel proud and happy for your child who made it onto the varsity basketball team when he comes to tell you the good news, his own face alight with unadulterated joy.

There are five key components of empathy: Understanding others, developing others, service orientation, leveraging diversity, and political awareness. These together combine to create the empathy that you feel for others. It is a skill that can be developed, though it should come naturally to some degree.

Understanding Others	• Involves sensing others' feelings and being interested in whatever concerns or needs the other person has.
Developing Others	• Involves acting to meet other people's needs or feelings
Service Orientation	• Involves putting others first and attempting to go out of your way to help others
Leveraging Diversity	• Recognizing both the differences between people's skills and the value in diversity for survival of the group
Political Awareness	• Involves responding to a group's emotional states, allowing for a group relationship to be fostered

The Purpose of Empathy

Empathy exists to keep us cognizant of others' needs. We use empathy to allow us to look at a person near us and understand how they are feeling, which in turn, cues us in on what that person may be needing at that particular moment. By understanding how someone is feeling through empathy, we are able to relate to other people within our social groups, and that motivates us to help them meet their own needs. It instills this sense of compassion within us that encourages us to tend to others and behave selflessly. This selflessness enables larger groups of people to survive. It is that inherent desire to ensure that your partners, friends, children, and other loved ones are cared for, which helps further ensure their own survival.

Empathy goes a step further in ensuring survival as well: It allows for labor to be tailored to individuals' strengths, fully expecting each to contribute to the society's survival in a meaningful fashion. Instead of each person having to go out and survive on his or her own without help, empathy, and society allows for each person to specialize. One person may hunt while another focuses on farming and yet another works on general construction and maintenance of the village. Someone else entirely may make the food that the hunter and farmer provide, and ultimately, everyone ends up with a variety of needs met while only having to specialize in one task. From an evolutionary standpoint, empathy is one of the main reasons humanity has developed as far as it has: People no longer have to do everything in order to survive and can instead specialize.

The doctor does not have to worry about hunting to make sure he has food so he can focus on medical care. The hunter does not have to worry about making clothing so she can focus solely on providing food. The teacher does not have to worry about food or shelter and can instead tend to children. In today's society, it takes a village to meet all needs, and empathy is what enables us to do so.

Empathy and Emotional Intelligence

Empathy is one of the key components of emotional intelligence. Empathy acts as the bond between yourself and those around you, and that ability to understand those around you as though you yourself were in his or her shoes. This enables you to deepen your bonds with other people, which can be the key to building a higher EQ. Consider the man who came home from work angry that was discussed in the introduction: Had he stopped and considered how the person with whom he had fought at work had felt, he may have been able to respond better. If the two of them fought over part of their work not being done because each believed the other would take care of it, the man could have stopped to consider that maybe his coworker had been confused and it was all a big misunderstanding. Through empathy, you are able to better control your own emotions because you are aware of how they impact those around you. You can see and feel the hurt you inflict when you act impulsively or out of anger or fear. Likewise, you feel good when those around you feel good, making you more interested in meeting the needs of others.

Understanding Temperament

Temperament describes an individual's nature: It is how he or she behaves naturally. It is primarily inherited genetically, creating traits that were either nurtured or developed early in life, or that came innately. Temperament is particularly tricky as it is a predisposition for a specific type of behavior, though it does not necessarily guarantee that whatever you are predisposed toward is going to happen. Here are four examples of temperament in action:

Shy	• Quiet, uncomfortable in groups, avoids being center of attention.
Stubborn	• Hard-headed, refuses to compromise, refuses to acknowledge being wrong
Athletic	• Competitive, active, strong, team player
Outgoing	• Enjoys attention, thrives with friends, seeks plenty of social situations

The Purpose of Temperament

Temperament provides your base personality. It is your inherent preferences and dislikes, how you react to crowds, whether you enjoy sports, how you react to certain stimuli, and so much more. Your temperament is essentially your basic foundation for your personality. You can be introverted or extroverted, athletic, stubborn, easygoing, submissive, or so many more different traits. The temperament serves that basis and dictates our reactions. Someone who is shy is not likely to enjoy herself at a school dance and will probably do anything possible to skip or leave early, whereas someone who is hardheaded and dominant is likely going to thrive in some sort of leadership position, and will actively avoid any situations that would require submission. Your temperament cues other people to respond to you in certain ways, while you likely take the same cues from other people's temperaments. The important part to remember is that while you can shape your own temperament, you cannot outright change it. While your temperament does influence your behavior, what it does is determine how you do something rather than what you choose to do. Your temperament is not an excuse for poor behavior, but it will provide you with insight to understand why you have the tendencies you do.

The Cause of Temperament

Temperament is believed to be largely inherited, but also is related to the environment in which you may find yourself and also life experience, particularly in the younger years. Together, genetics or biological predispositions, physical attributes, environment, and early life experiences come together to form your temperament. Someone with a biological predisposition toward caution or anxiety who is born into a stressful environment and spent much of early childhood crying as parents argued is likely to grow into an anxious person, whereas that same child could have been generally happy but somewhat cautious or slow to warm up to situations had the parents been less combative and the home more relaxed and encouraging in the early years. Overall, the four traits combine and create a person's base personality or temperament.

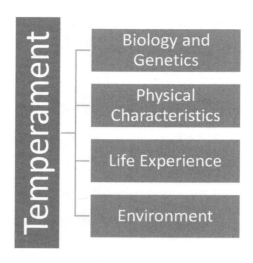

The Relevance of Temperament to Emotional Intelligence

Those who have a lower EQ are typically enslaved to their temperament. Their EQ may not be enough to mitigate damaging or destructive behaviors, and they react emotionally instead of rationally. They will almost always behave in ways that come naturally thanks to their temperament. This is not always a good thing: The shy person becomes unable to overcome her fear of social events and may struggle in formal professional or academic settings.

The hardheaded person may ruin relationships due to being entirely unwilling to compromise or admit when he is wrong. These can lead to catastrophic results in which the people are unsuccessful and unhappy with their lives, and the people around them are equally as unhappy.

On the other hand, people with higher levels of emotional intelligence are able to more or less override their base temperaments. While they, as a whole, are still shy or hardheaded, they are able to work past those temperaments to do what they need to do.

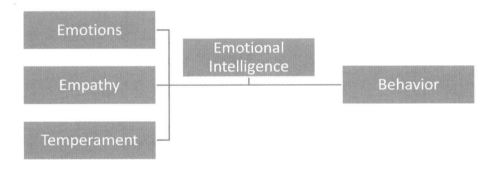

The shy person may be a fantastic HR director, despite hating social interaction, because she is able to look past that anxiety she feels when confronted with people or problems and instead, with empathy and compassion, decides to help other people rather than cave to her own introverted nature. The hardheaded man may hate conceding, but be willing to do so when he can rationalize that he is, in fact, wrong. By having higher levels of emotional intelligence, people are able to acknowledge their feelings and their temperaments for what they are, but they are able to use the rational part of their minds to overcome them when necessary or when it is beneficial to do so.

Chapter 2: Emotional Intelligence

We are all born with an inherent understanding of basic emotions. Even deaf and blind babies who may never have been exposed to sound or seeing a smile naturally show emotions the same way as grown adults: They cry when they need something or are afraid and smile at things that make them happy. This capacity for understanding and expressing emotions is hardwired into them in order to help them survive, and that understanding is used constantly.

You naturally seek to read other people's emotions in every interaction you have. Have you ever approached someone who appeared to be in a foul mood and felt that moment of apprehension toward interacting with him or her? Or have you ever seen someone so happy that you could not help but smile and feel a little more at ease? Your mind unconsciously reads the body language of everyone around you, responding to the tiniest differences in expressions and the positions of the body, whether someone is tense with their head up or down, where the hands are, and so on. That instant understanding at a glance comes from emotional intelligence. It helps us navigate society without stepping on other people's emotional toes left and right, and helps enable us to live as a successful society and ensure that everyone's needs are met.

Defining Emotional Intelligence

Simply put, emotional intelligence is the ability to regulate the emotions of yourself and others, being able to accurately define other people's emotions, and using emotional feedback to influence your own thoughts and behaviors, as well as the behaviors of others. You are able to recognize your own emotional states and use that feedback to guide your reactions in order to make the best possible decisions on what kinds of behaviors you should exhibit. You are able to control your own emotions and utilize them to ensure that your own needs are met. It also allows you to handle your relationships with other people with tact, which betters interpersonal relationships.

Further simplified, emotional intelligence is being aware of the fact that emotions have a massive amount influence on everything you do. Your own thoughts and behaviors are heavily influenced by your emotions and recognizing that while being able to keep your own emotions in check enables you to behave in ways that are conducive to fixing problems that may be influencing your emotions in a negative manner.

Emotional intelligence, when all aspects are combined, create leaders. People with high EQs in each of the main constructs of emotional intelligence are typically much better at leadership roles than those with lower EQs. Each of the constructs combine to create a well-rounded individual that is concerned with the welfare of those around him or her, able to balance the needs of those around him or her, and able to manage everyone and motivate them to act in ways that are conducive to the group's success as a whole.

Importance of Emotional Intelligence

You may be asking yourself why emotional intelligence matters. If you are able to innately understand basic emotions and those emotions have very specific purposes, why does it matter whether you can influence them? If they are evolutionarily important, why override them? Would that not be counterproductive to our very nature as human beings? Yes and no; emotions are important and should be given consideration as they often have very important implications, but at the same time, if all we do is give in to our emotions, which are, all things considered, quite fickle, we become impulsive and unproductive. Relationships suffer when we respond to people because we were momentarily angry at them. We say things in anger that we may not mean. Sadness and grief can be completely crippling if we act upon them. Happiness and enjoyment can lead to destructive behaviors such as drug abuse, but can also destroy careers if all you ever do is what makes you happy with no regard to responsibilities. Fear can render you paralyzed when what you need to do is act in order to save yourself or others you care about.

These emotions are important biologically, but humans have developed to the point that we can think critically and rationally. If we only reacted based on emotions, we would be crippling our own potential. Think of how a toddler behaves: He is likely impulsive and gives in to every feeling that passes, as that is all he knows. He does not know how to control his emotions, and his need for instant gratification leads to all sorts of trouble. Toddlers may hit, scream, throw temper tantrums, steal, or put themselves in danger impulsively. They do not have that capacity for rational thought that humans develop throughout early adulthood. Denying that rationality and refusing to act upon it is to deny humanity itself. You have developed the ability to understand the relationships between how you feel, your general temperament, the situation at hand, and your behaviors, and you are able to influence that with rational thought.

Being able to influence all of your behaviors with rational thought means you are not a slave to instinct. You can act selflessly to aid someone else, though your instincts are screaming at you to leave. You can be a leader that recognizes the feelings of everyone around you and leads with compassion and empathy rather than through dominance. Your behaviors are the keys to all interpersonal relationships, and when you can control those behaviors with high EQ, you can better influence your relationships and be more successful in social situations. High EQ allows you to be more efficient at resolving conflicts, and empathize better with others. By having better relationships with those around you, you are more likely to be happy and relaxed. You are more likely to be healthier, both physically and mentally, because you are happier in your relationships and more secure in your place in society.

Ultimately, there is not a single aspect of your life that is not touched in some way by emotional intelligence. It impacts everything, whether you are conscious of it or not. EQ influences your success both socially and professionally; sometimes more than IQ does, and understanding its importance is critical to understanding why developing a higher EQ is so crucial to being successful in life.

Applications of Emotional Intelligence

Understanding how EQ can impact various aspects of relationships is crucial to seeing just how profoundly it can impact your life. This section will provide what high EQ looks like in each of the following situations and contrast it with what may happen when someone with lower EQ is also in the same situation. The difference between the two can be staggering when compared side-by-side.

EQ in Romantic Relationships

Imagine you and your spouse are arguing again. Your spouse is a stay at home parent to young children while you work full time during standard office hours. Each day, you come home, and your spouse asks for help as soon as you walk in the door. You can see that your spouse looks stressed, still wearing dirty pajamas, dinner is on the stove, cooking, and the living room looks like a bomb exploded with toys. The children are bickering, and your spouse quickly shoves the children at you and hands you the spatula before disappearing to the bathroom, shutting and locking the door and turning on the shower.

Assuming you have a lower EQ, you may immediately get angry. After all, you have just come home from work, and you are mentally drained from a day of office work. Your spouse got to stay home, you tell yourself angrily, and it looks as though your spouse has gotten nothing done all day. The home is trashed, the children are not fed, and dinner is not finished. In your anger, you follow your spouse to the bathroom and proceed to yell through the door. You do not recognize that your spouse had looked stressed prior to leaving or consider that all that your spouse had heard all day was the sound of the very children bickering that was skyrocketing your own anger. The children hear you screaming through the door and run away to cry. Your spouse does not open the door. Dinner burns on the stove. All of that compounds on your anger and makes it worse. Your relationships with both your spouse and your children have been harmed. Your spouse feels as though you are not supportive, and your children learn to avoid you because you are an angry person.

Stop and think about how the situation would have played out had you had a higher EQ. You would have walked through the door and seen the desperation painted across your spouse's face. You would have been able to feel the stress, and anxiety practically emanating from your spouse and see how overwhelmed your spouse was with the situation. Instead of getting angry, you would have seen that what your spouse needed was a quick reprieve from the constant nagging of children. You would have happily entertained the children, and the change in pace may have been enough to stop their bickering. You would have finished up dinner, getting it plated and serving the children, who happily ran to eat. Your spouse would have emerged from the shower feeling much more at ease and ready to tackle the rest of the evening, and would have felt supported and loved because you had taken the initiative to alleviate some of the stress. Your relationship, instead of being hurt, was strengthened by your ability to deescalate the situation. Furthermore, your children learn that marriage is a partnership. The tit-for-tat sort of comparison is harmful, and what a marriage needs is for both partners to look out for each other's needs, even when they are not verbally expressed, and even when they may not be convenient.

EQ in Familial Relationships

Imagine that your children have been misbehaving all day. They keep running through the house, as children do when they are cooped up indoors due to bad weather, and no matter how often you tell them to stop, you can hear the thudding of their quick footsteps running down the hallway again minutes later. After the umpteenth time of reminding them to stop and enjoying the momentary reprieve from the constant thumps of their feet, you hear their running start again, followed by a loud bang, and glass shattering. You rush out and see that your children because they were not listening, ran into the hutch and knocked out an entire row of wine glasses, which shattered all over the floor.

Assuming you have low EQ, you are likely to run out and yell. Immediately you scream at the children for not listening, chewing them out for their disobedience ruining everything and telling them to look at the mess they left for you. Despite the fear, pain, and guilt on their faces, you belittle them for not listening, say something along the lines of accusing them of not being good kids or wishing they were not there, and you yell at them both to go to their rooms for the rest of the night. Your children stare at you in horror for a moment before breaking down into tears and running away. You ignored the fact that one of the children had a cut on her foot and the other was terrified of you, and you ignored the damage that your outburst had to your children. As your children aged, they sought to put more and more distance between you and them, until they eventually left and cut off contact due to your abusive tendencies during their childhood.

With higher EQ, you would have ran out to see what happened, and immediately ask if your children are okay. You would have surveyed them, picked each up out of the glass, and taken them to the other room to patch them up while having a serious, but still calm, conversation about this being the reason you asked them not to play so roughly indoors. Instead of losing your temper, you used the incident to teach the children a lesson. When they were all patched up, you took them back to the mess and asked them to help you clean it up in an age-appropriate manner. Each child contributed to the mess, and they each sincerely apologized. You gave your children hugs, reminded them that you love them, and told them sternly to avoid running indoors. They nodded and left to go play by themselves, feeling secure in their attachment to you, and having learned a very valuable lesson. You strengthened your relationship with your children, and they have learned that they can rely on you in moments of need thanks to your level-headed response to what was a messy situation.

EQ in Platonic Relationships

Imagine that you are setting up for your friend to come over to your house for an evening of video games, a few beers, and some pizza. It is a very low-key event meant to be relaxing. The time that your friend was supposed to arrive came and went, and almost an hour later, he finally shows up. He looks upset about something and mutters an apology, but entirely avoids the topic of why he was late. Instead, he grabs a beer, sits down silently to watch you play the game. He downs the beer and then grabs another without a word. He glances at his phone off and on, his expression darkening every time he does.

If you have a lower EQ, you may respond to this negatively. You are hurt that your friend was late and offered no apology or explanation. You are angry that you feel devalued. You are sad that your friend seems to not care that you are feeling upset about his actions. Instead of looking at him and seeing his own feelings, you look at him and snap. You tell him that if he doesn't want to be there, and it looks like that is the case, then he can just leave because you do not need his negativity bringing down the mood when you wanted to have a good time. You tell him off for checking his phone so often and tell him that he is an awful friend and that you refuse to put up with such disrespect. In response, your friend does not say a word. He picks up his phone, looks as though he might cry, and walks out. He never texts you again, never answers when you call and refuses to acknowledge you every time you ever see him out and about. He ended the friendship over your outburst.

With a higher EQ, you may have looked at the situation and seen that your friend was not doing well. At a glance, you would have been able to see the hurt in his expression upon walking through your door, and you would have been more willing to provide him with the support he must have needed. Despite the annoyance you felt, you also understood that your friend was not doing well, and that superseded your annoyance. Even if he did not want to talk about what had happened, you would have seen that what he really needed in that moment was to be supp0rted during some sort of personal struggle. Instead of putting him down, you would have patiently waited for him to share whatever had happened, and while you waited, you would have continued gaming and genuinely enjoying your friend's company. Eventually, he would eventually open up about having a fight with his fiancée prior to leaving to see you, and he would thank you for being such a great friend.

EQ in Workplace Relationships

Imagine you are at work. You have a group project that you and your coworkers have been working on for the last month. The day before the project is to be submitted, you all realize that no-one worked on a specific portion of the project that was incredibly important, and without it, your project cannot be submitted. Each of you thought that part of the project was going to be completed by another person, and nobody checked on it until the day before it was due when you were all putting together the project so you could go over the final project. The final piece for the project is rather time-consuming.

With a lower EQ, you may explode on your coworkers. You may yell about it not being finished and assign blame to the other people around you, seeking any explanation that would remove blame from yourself. You say that it was clearly your coworker Mary's fault because she was supposed to do something else related to it. You may yell some words that are not appropriate in the workplace, and that causes you to get in trouble with HR. The assignment is never worked on. Further, you all are reprimanded for failing to complete the requirements, and you find yourself without a job due to the situation escalating so badly.

With a higher EQ, you may have been angry, and you may have seen the frustration on everyone else's faces, but instead of giving in to that anger and frustration, you instead chose to analyze the situation. You looked over what was still needed, and while it would be a lot for an individual person to complete, you point out that it is something that you can all finish relatively quickly if you each take a segment of it. Everyone in your group looks to you to hear you out, and soon, the mood seems to calm. Your coworkers follow your lead, and within a few hours, you all have completed the remaining work together. Your project is submitted on time, and everyone is thrilled with the outcome. You feel happy and fulfilled because you managed to turn a bad situation into a good one, and your coworkers feel as though you are trustworthy and like they can count on you when things get tough. The next time you all have a project, you are designated the leader who is in charge of making sure everyone has a role and that everything is being completed. This newfound admiration from coworkers betters your reputation with your bosses, and soon, you find yourself with a raise and promotion due to your tact and emotional intelligence.

EQ in Social Situations

Imagine you are at a big party. You have always been a bit more reserved and hate going to events like this, but you were pressured into going by one of your friends. The party is loud, obnoxious, and everyone around you is drinking, something you are not comfortable doing in public. One person walks by, clearly intoxicated, and trips and spills a beer right down your shirt. He slurs out an apology and continues on his way, leaving you drenched in beer in the middle of a party that you did not want to attend in the first place.

With lower EQ, you may look at your friend for a moment before exploding. You scream about how you did not want to attend the party in the first place. You tell your friend that next time, he should listen to you, and you throw down the drink you had been handed before storming out. Quickly, the party seems to quiet down as all eyes are on you. They watch as you leave, and the party seems to die down. Your friend awkwardly watches as you leave, and within the next few days, news of your outburst in the middle of the party spreads throughout your peers, tarnishing your reputation. People stop wanting to talk to you or invite you places, and the friend that you had yelled at seems less interested in continuing your friendship.

With a higher level of EQ, you may have stopped, been frustrated, but then recognized that it was an accident. You would not have allowed your prior annoyance at not wanting to be there to cause you to blow up. Instead, you would have quietly excused yourself to clean up without making a scene or destroying someone's flooring at a party.

You would have found something to do with your friend and tried to enjoy yourself, even if you would have rather been doing something else. By not being sucked into your anger, you are still able to find enjoyment in other things. You may even be able to make some new friends or try new things. Regardless of whether you eventually find something worthwhile, by not reacting volatilely, you are able to keep from overreacting and hurting people around you.

Chapter 3: The Emotional Intelligence Framework

Emotional intelligence is composed of several different skills that make you capable of understanding and appraising emotions, regardless of whether they are your own or belonging to other people. People with higher EQ are typically much more effective at controlling and regulating their feelings, which enables individuals to better control behaviors.

Breaking down Emotional Intelligence

Emotional intelligence is better understood by breaking it down beyond understanding what it is as a whole. The entirety of emotional intelligence is comprised of five separate realms of emotional intelligence, which are further organized into four quadrants that affect each other. Understanding these ways of breaking down and organizing emotional intelligence is useful in understanding where you stand and what the purpose of each of the skills is.

Realms of Emotional Intelligence

The skills of emotional intelligence can be broken down into five separate realms or behaviors and skills:

- *Understanding your emotions*
- *Regulating your emotions*
- *Keeping yourself motivated*
- *Understanding and recognizing the emotions of other people*
- *Managing relationships* (managing the emotions of other people)

Each of these realms of emotional intelligence is important, but being strong in one does not necessarily mean you are emotionally intelligent, nor does it mean that you will be particularly effective in social situations. In order to be emotionally intelligent, you must be proficient in all five realms. Someone who understands and controls his emotions with no regard for other people's emotions is not going to be emotionally intelligent; everything he does will be to ensure that his own needs are met. Likewise, someone who is skilled at understanding and recognizing other people's emotions but is awful at self-regulation of emotions is going to be selfless to a fault and find that her needs are never met. All five realms come together to create one well-rounded, emotionally intelligent person.

Quadrants of Emotional Intelligence

The four quadrants or domains of emotional intelligence are:

- *Self-Awareness*
- *Self-Management*
- *Social Awareness*
- *Relationship Management*

As you can see, each of these closely relates to one of the realms of emotional intelligence. Each of these skills can be sorted onto a chart to represent a different combination of self or social-relational and awareness or regulation.

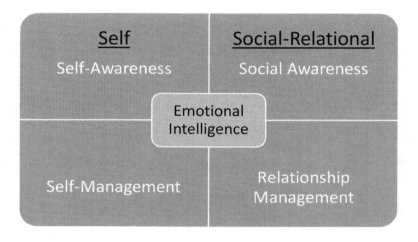

Each quadrant of emotional intelligence relates closely to the others. A high self-awareness typically lends itself to higher social awareness and self-management. When you have a higher social awareness and self-management, you are more likely to have stronger relationship management skills. When all four quadrants are strongly developed, that person is believed to be very emotionally intelligent.

Self-Awareness

Within emotional intelligence, self-awareness involves developing a deeper understanding of your own emotions. It involves knowing yourself and understanding what you are feeling or need. If you are able to identify and meet the needs of yourself, you are far more likely to be able to understand and meet the needs of other people. For this reason, the foundation of emotional intelligence begins with self-awareness.

Some traits associated with self-awareness include the following:

- Being self-confident because you understand yourself
- Being aware of your own strengths and weaknesses
- Being conscious of your current emotional state
- Understanding how your actions affect other people
- Understanding and being conscious of how other people or situations influence your own emotional state

By having a deep understanding of yourself, you have the foundation to understanding others. After all, if you could not identify when you are sad, how could you possibly hope to recognize sadness in another person? Without the most fundamental basics of emotions and how they impact you, you will struggle to ever truly relate to other people.

Low Self-Awareness

There are several signs that may point that you have a low self-awareness quotient. If you feel like you have any of these signs, you may need to work on your self-awareness.

- Easily stressed: When you are not in control of your emotions and not doing what is necessary to cope with the negative ones, you may find yourself easily stressed out by things that would not be a big deal to someone with a higher EQ. If you are not addressing your emotions as they come up due to a lack of knowledge to do so, you are going to see it build up and stress you out.

- Difficulty being assertive: People lacking the EQ necessary often struggle to handle conflict in a productive manner. Instead, they resort to passive or aggressive behavior to allow the conflict to pass.

- Struggle to describe emotional states: People who cannot label specific emotions as they feel them struggle to handle them. For example, while they may be able to identify that they feel bad, they cannot label whether what they are feeling is anxiety, frustration, or sadness.

- Operate on assumptions: People lacking in EQ often make a snap decision or assumption and then fall victim to the fallacy of confirmation bias; they will accept any evidence supporting their opinion while ignoring the evidence that contradicts it.

- Hold grudges: Grudges come from stress responses, and people lacking in EQ struggle to cope with that stress.

- Lock onto mistakes: People with lower EQs frequently lock onto their mistakes and refuse to look past them, or they forget about them, dooming them to repeat the same mistakes over and over again.

- Feeling misunderstood: People with lower EQs cannot clearly convey their own emotions because they do not understand them themselves, leaving plenty of room for misinterpretation.
- Lack of understanding what your emotional triggers are: Everyone has some sort of trigger— something that immediately causes strong, and often irrational responses to some sort of stimulus. Those lacking in EQ often do not know what theirs are.
- Hiding emotions: People with lower EQs tend to see negative emotions poorly and instead prefer to keep them hidden behind positive ones. This means that their needs are never being addressed because they are never using their negative emotions.
- Blaming others for how they make you feel: People with lower EQs see other people as responsible for triggering their own emotional responses instead of recognizing that no one is responsible for their emotional states.
- Being easily offended: Those with lower EQ typically lack the self-confidence those with higher

EQs have. They also lack the understanding of their own strengths and weaknesses, which makes them a little more self-conscious when called out for them.

Self-Management

Self-management involves the ability to dictate your own thoughts, feelings, and behaviors. This quadrant of emotional intelligence focuses on your ability to manage yourself. It includes your responses to those around you and the situations you may find yourself in, as well as expressing your positive emotions while controlling negative reactions. While negative emotions are acceptable to feel, they should never be in control of you as a person. You should be able to manage feeling negative feelings while still not harming others or lashing out. It involves using self-awareness to keep those negative feelings within your control, as you are able to identify what they are and why you are feeling them.

Some of the frequently seen abilities in people with high self-management include:

- Keeping control of emotions: The ability to recognize and feel emotions without letting them dictate behaviors.

- Trustworthy: These people are reliable and often make it a point to follow through with what they have agreed to do.
- Flexible: The ability to roll with change when it is unexpectedly comes up without it ruining the plans or stopping the individual from meeting other goals.
- Optimistic: Negative feelings are not enough to discourage him or her from attempting to achieve desired results.
- Motivated to achieve goals: Knowing what is desired and motivated to make that happen.
- Willing to take initiative: Comfortable being the one initiating change and

Low Self-Management
- Struggle to control emotions: People with lower self-management struggle to keep their own feelings, and therefore their own actions, under control. They typically respond emotionally rather than rationally.

- Struggle to take criticisms: Anything negative said toward those with low self-management struggle to keep their disappointment or other negative emotions in control after feeling criticized.

- Cannot cope with change or the unexpected: Those with lower self-management struggle when things do not go according to plans. Coping with the change is difficult, as change or the unexpected typically come with stronger negative emotions.

- Impulsive: Those with lower self-management struggle to keep their impulses under control. When given the chance, they will take something that they like better, even if it has a worse consequence. The consequence does not matter nearly as much as the happiness from going along with the impulse.

- Need instant gratification: Oftentimes, people with lower self-management tend to go with gratification sooner rather than waiting for a better result. For example, they are likely to go through with buying something they cannot afford with cash and put it on a credit card where they will pay significant amounts of interest if the alternative is waiting for months to be able to afford to pay cash. They'd rather have the item sooner, even if the consequence is worse.

Social Awareness

Social awareness focuses on understanding what other people want and need. It is the ability to look at someone else and understand how they feel or what they need in that particular moment. Those who are socially aware can tell at a glance how they should approach another person and how to keep situations calm. They oftentimes go out of their way to meet the needs of other people just because they feel as though they can, so they should. Oftentimes, they exhibit some of these traits:

- Empathetic: A deep understanding of how someone else feels and what is needed in the moment.
- An understanding of group structures: They recognize how society works and the idea of give-and-take communities in which everyone contributes something.
- Service-oriented: They prioritize other people's needs and wants in order to ensure that they are met as much as possible.

When you have a high level of social awareness, you are able to consider other people's wants and needs effectively and meet those needs quickly. These people frequently excel at being leaders or public speakers: They excel at speaking in the way that the people want to hear and use that skill to gain the support they need at their jobs. These people are typically quite charismatic, but also selfless in the sense that they are doing their best to ensure that others' needs are being considered. Social awareness requires a developed sense of self-awareness to really be effective.

Low Social Awareness

- Untrusting: Those who lack social awareness typically do not trust those around them, nor do they earn the trust of those around them. By never meeting other people's needs, they never establish themselves as trustworthy.

- Lack empathy: When lacking social awareness, it is quite difficult to understand what other people are feeling. They struggle to relate to other people meaningfully because they cannot deeply understand the other people's needs.

- Selfish: When social awareness and empathy do not play a role in life, people do not feel the pressure to ensure that other people's needs are met.

- Manipulative: Those without much social awareness do not feel bad about using other people in order to get what they want. Their lack of empathy means they do not care as much about hurting other people.

- Closed-minded: Social awareness allows for thoughts of diversity and understanding how every person, no matter how different, can contribute in some way. Those lacking in social awareness may not see the use of some people's skills or understand how nonessential jobs or skills may still contribute to the overall wellbeing of society.

- Isolated: Because those lacking social awareness do not trust others and lack sophisticated empathy, they typically retreat to be by themselves rather than associating with other people. They do not build up social support groups and instead live on their own.

Relationship Management

Relationship management is the most complex of the four quadrants of emotional intelligence. It involves the ability to influence other people through your own words and actions, allowing for inspiration, and the ability to mediate and solve conflicts that may arise within the groups you are inspiring. This is the ultimate trait for leaders: It is what enables you to lead effectively and kindly, earning that position as opposed to having to take it through domination. Those with high relationship management skills make conscious decisions about their interactions with others so they can get a desired outcome that best suits the needs at that moment.

1. **Make a decision** about the best way to proceed in the current situation. You have taken the time to analyze how those around you are feeling, as well as identifying the reasons for those feelings. From there, you will decide what the most effective ways to interact with those around you are, as well as considering the potential reactions you may get based on how you approach them. You will also

consider how their reactions will affect you and have plans and skills in place to manage those potentially negative feelings effectively and appropriately.

2. **Interact with others** in the way that you have determined is the best possible course of actions. These interactions can vary in form. For example, it could be written or verbal, and with a single person or the entire group.

3. **Identify an outcome** you desire and tailor your interactions to that outcome. You will interact with the people in ways that you know will influence them to create the outcome you desire, adding an intentional element to the act of relationship management.

4. **Identify the needs** you are trying to meet in order to be sure that the outcome is the right one for the situation. You want your outcome to meet the needs of yourself, the people around you, or whatever the needs your decision is addressing are at that particular moment.

People with high skills in relationship management typically exhibit the following traits:

- Influential
- Inspirational
- Invested in the development of other people
- Willing to be the catalyst for changes
- Acting as the conflict mediator
- Cultivating and encouraging bonds between the people within the group
- Create teams that work well together and encourage teamwork or collaboration

Low Relationship Management

- Ineffective leader: Those who struggle with relationship management fail at being in leadership roles. They are typically too self-absorbed or socially blind to understand the nuances behind leading a group effectively
- Untrusted and disliked: Typically, those with low relationship management struggle to prove themselves trustworthy or likeable. People prefer to avoid them.

- Act selfishly: They may fail to acknowledge other people's needs, or simply do not care about others' needs for other reasons. Regardless, they do not inspire much loyalty when they refuse to help others.

- Are uninspiring: No matter how much they may ask other people to help them or do something, people do not feel motivated, obligated, or a desire to do as they were asked.

- Likely see a constant revolving door of new employees or relationships: Because these people struggle with relationships, they are frequently seeing new ones, either at work or in their personal lives. This constant refresh of people in the person's life mean he or she never really learns to develop meaningful relationships.

Interrelationship of Emotional Intelligence Components.

Within emotional intelligence, all four quadrants are interrelated. They build upon each other to create a well-rounded, emotionally intelligent individual. The basic foundation is formed by self-awareness; having a certain degree of self-awareness provides you with the ability to begin thinking about both self-management and social awareness. If you struggle with self-awareness, you are likely to struggle to move to the next step of self-management or social awareness. Oftentimes, self-awareness is one of the best places to begin practicing and strengthening your emotional intelligence, as the others require the skills developed through self-awareness to be effective at the others.

Self-Awareness | Self-Management and Social Awareness | Relationship Management

After self-awareness is developed, self-management and social awareness become possible. You cannot manage yourself and your emotions if you lack a basic understanding of what your emotions are or how they work, and likewise, if you are unaware of your own feelings, you cannot hope to understand how someone else is feeling or what they may need. Developing both self-management and social awareness leads to an ability to begin developing relationship management. Without self-awareness, the entire process of developing emotional intelligence becomes increasingly more difficult. It takes a mastery of self-awareness, self-management, and social awareness to begin to learn relationship management.

Part II:
Emotional Intelligence Tests
and Assessment

Chapter 4: What is an Emotional Intelligence Test?

Imagine that you have just been fired from yet another job. You had always done your best at work but tried to keep to yourself. You did not care when people around you were struggling to complete their work, and even when you were free at that particular moment, you rarely extended an offer for work. Because you never developed many trusting relationships at work or went above and beyond, people were not particularly interested in helping you, either. One day, you were struggling to catch up on your work, and despite your best efforts, you could just not keep up. No one around you offered to help you, as you had never offered to help any of them, and eventually, you blew up at work. You could not take another moment of listening to two of your coworkers chattering right outside your cubicle, and in a moment of rage, you yelled at them to either make themselves useful and help you or get away from your desk. You may have even sprinkled in a few swears during your rant. Ultimately, you were fired and left wondering why, after all that time of you being a good employee who did the job and never caused trouble before, you were let go. Sure, you had one blow up, but everyone has a bad day sometimes, and that should have been excused considering your track record. This seemed to happen everywhere you went: You would go, do your job, keep to yourself, and ultimately be let go when you were doing your job regularly, and you could not understand why. Through some web searching, you found your answer: A lack of emotional intelligence.

You may be doing your job on a regular basis, but you have proven that you are not a team player in that particular situation. Workplaces want to build teams of people who work well together and will help each other when the need arises, not people who do the bare minimum to get their own work done while letting other people suffer the consequences of not having their work finished. With your newfound understanding of the value of emotional intelligence, you begin searching for how to improve it.

Ultimately, you feel lost. You may know that you struggle with anxiety sometimes, or that your ability to meet others' needs could use some work. Despite knowing this, you may have no idea where to begin or how to decide where to continue working on yourself. You know that you would like to be an emotionally intelligent person because emotionally intelligent people seem to do better in a wider range of situations, but are unsure of how to attain it or where you may need to improve yourself. Luckily for you, this is exactly why emotional intelligence tests exist!

Whether you want a general idea just for fun, or you are serious about understanding where you fall on the scale of emotional intelligence, taking a test can be a fantastic way to get that picture. While these may not always be accurate due to the way they are executed and because they rely on self-reporting of situations and moods, they still provide great general information that can point you in the right direction on your journey toward emotional intelligence.

Just as how IQ tests exist, there are also tests designed to quantify levels of emotional intelligence. These tests typically consist of several questions designed to assess your strengths and skills in emotional intelligence to create a hard number to represent your EQ. The tests can be crucial tools to understanding where your emotional strengths and weaknesses are, and can provide a more thorough understanding of yourself as an individual. These tests can come in a variety of forms, ranging from true or false questions, questions that ask you to quantify how much something describes you or the frequency of a behavior or can be verbal questions at an interview designed to gauge your emotional intelligence.

How EQ Is Tested

Typically, EQ is tested through a series of questions. You will be given a sort of quiz with a series of situations and circumstances, and you must identify how you would react or whether it describes you. The goal is for you to identify as honestly as possible to create the most accurate assessment that can be created. Each question created to test an individual's EQ creates a situation in which there are several reactions possible and assigns each possible reaction a score in relation to a specific quadrant of emotional intelligence. For example, a question testing self-awareness would likely question one's own reactions in certain situations regarding being stressed, overwhelmed, or otherwise negatively influenced by emotion, often in a way that can assign a value. For example, you may see a question that asks if you do not let your emotions get the best of you, with the choices you are provided being "always," "sometimes," "rarely," and "never." Always would score 4 points while never scored a 0. This allows for a quantifiable assessment of your ability to control your emotions.

The tests frequently ask a series of questions for each quadrant of emotional intelligence, and at the end, they add them up and divide the scores into several categories to use to provide your results. If you score in the top percentile, you are said to have high intelligence in that category, while average scores mean it could use some work, and low scores implying that you need serious effort in that particular category.

Together, you are able to add your questions together and see where you score.

Sometimes, workplaces will perform EQ tests during interviews when seeking to hire or promote people. In those cases, the test is most frequently done verbally, with an emphasis on understanding your own personal reactions to certain scenarios, or with you providing a time that you had a conflict at work and asking how you may have resolved it. You will often be given a question, and then allowed a few moments to consider it before being expected to answer it.

These questions typically relate to empathy or conflict resolution, and they are some of the most important questions at your interview. If your interviewer is asking you questions to judge emotional intelligence, then they are oftentimes specifically seeking out someone with emotional intelligence, even if that person is not the most qualified academically or experientially.

Why Test for EQ?

As discussed, emotional intelligence has a strong impact in virtually every aspect of your life. Understanding your EQ allows you to identify your strengths and weaknesses, which can be incredibly useful when it comes to recognizing your behaviors for what they are. You need to understand your weaknesses if you hope to compensate for them and begin to work on filling them in to prevent them from being problematic in the future. Your own relationships and general wellbeing will increase if you can raise your EQ, as you will become generally better at managing yourself and your emotional reactions. By bettering your control over yourself, you are able to avoid falling for the traps that many people do in communicating with others: Giving in to anger. You will be able to recognize your anger and use it to fuel your desire to fix the situation without lashing out or making the situation worse for yourself or others. You may find that your problem was a simple miscommunication, and someone who is emotionally intelligent can take that information and learn from it to ensure it is not a problem again in the future.

Beyond testing EQ to understand yourself, it is sometimes tested in other situations as well. Sometimes, interviews for jobs involve questions that test for emotional intelligence. It has been found that some of the best performing people in many different careers have higher EQs, even if they are less intellectually intelligent than some of the lesser-performing individuals. Ultimately, EQ has proven more accurate in determining success in workplaces than IQ.

Because high EQ is a better predictor of a good employee, many managers have begun using those questions to weed out people who are less emotionally intelligent and more likely to cause issues in the workplace. They ask questions that provide the hiring managers a better understanding of the interviewee's ability to recognize and regulate their own and others' emotions and behaviors, especially when needed to adapt to various workplace environments and situations. Employers want empathetic employees that are team players, great at communication, and well-equipped to handle a wide range of challenges or roadblocks that may be encountered during the work week.

Higher levels of social and emotional intelligence are important in a workplace, as those who are more emotionally intelligent place more of an emphasis on empathy, which means they will be there in support of their coworkers. If they see a coworker struggling, they are more likely to go forward and offer to help solve the problem than someone who does not see empathy as a major motivator. Those with higher emotional intelligence are also more in tune with their own strengths and weaknesses and are more receptive to feedback and constructive criticism than someone who struggles with their confidence.

What to Expect in an EQ Test

When taking an EQ test, you should expect to see a wide range of questions on various subjects. Some may be quite sensitive, such as asking about your own personal confidence levels, whereas others may seek to identify whether you are able to resolve conflicts or put other people's needs in front of your own. The tests are typically rather boring, and provide a series of similar questions, though they do have slightly different purposes for your score. You may see questions about your own emotions, as well as your interpretation of others emotions in similar circumstances, or you may seek questions that seek to measure how well you cope with the unexpected. Regardless of what the questions are, they all serve one purpose: To identify your weaknesses when it comes to emotional intelligence.

When you take a test, you must be honest. It is often helpful for people to go with their gut reactions when reading a question, as that gut reaction is typically the most accurate. Do not answer the test based on what you think may be the right or wrong answer, as all that will do is skew your data. If you want your test to be as accurate as possible and give you the most straightforward information about yourself, you must answer truthfully, even if you know it is an answer that would be attributed to a lower level of emotional intelligence. EQ is flexible and can be strengthened, so you should want the most accurate picture painted when taking the test. That accurate picture will be your roadmap to becoming more emotionally intelligent.

While the questions do not necessarily have to be taken in any specific amount of time, it helps to do them in one sitting if you can. You should be free of distractions when you begin your test, and you should make sure you have an ample amount of time free to tend to it. Some of the tests available can take up to an hour, though the one you will be provided in this book will be much shorter. You want to be able to focus on your questions within the same mindset and without other things distracting you that could potentially make you misunderstand the question or your own answer to it.

You should expect the questions to be easy enough to understand, though they may be about situations or traits about yourself that you have never considered. Give yourself a quick moment to consider them, and then write down the answer. Again, make sure that you provide your own honest answers to the questions rather than how someone else would answer for you. The important part is your own opinions and interpretations of yourself, especially because two of the quadrants are about yourself, and the basis of the entire emotional intelligence structure requires your own self-awareness.

Lastly, you should expect that this test will not be 100% accurate! As it relies wholly on self-reporting and involves questions on emotions, which are widely variable between people, you should take this as a general guide rather than as a diagnosis for what kind of person you are. It can absolutely point out your strengths and weaknesses, but you should make sure you take you understanding of the results as general assessments as opposed to being official assessments of your own emotional intelligence.

Sample Questions and Answers

The following questions and answers will be considered from the same hypothetical scenario introduced at the beginning of this chapter in which you imagine that you have been fired from your job after doing the bare minimum to meet your own job description without helping others at work and eventually having an outburst. Each question that will be provided will have an explanation of what it is testing for as well as the answer that the hypothetical you would provide, and what it would score if it were a part of this test.

Sample 1:

I am able to control myself when angry and keep myself from saying things I will later regret.

    1. Never

    2. Rarely

    3. Sometimes

    4. Often

    5. Always

You may have circled often here, with the reason being that oftentimes, you are able to control your anger. It is when you are already stressed out prior to being set off that you really struggle to control it and frequently say things in anger that you do not mean.

This question seeks to quantify self-management. It is asking you a question about your own feelings and your own behaviors to identify whether you are able to control yourself. One of the key facets of self-management is the ability to regulate your emotionally charged reactions, even when faced with the temptation to allow your emotions to rule you.

The answer never earns you 0 points, rarely earns 1, sometimes earns 2, often earns 3, and always earns 4 points toward emotional quotients. By answering that you can often control your anger, you earned 3 points toward your EQ.

Sample 2:

I understand what makes me angry most of the time.

1. *Never*
2. *Rarely*

3. *Sometimes*

4. *Often*

5. *Always*

You may have looked at this question and circled 3. You know some of the things that make you angry, such as when you feel the pressure to perform at work, but sometimes, you do find yourself angry without knowing why, and you have noticed that it can cause issues in your relationships.

This question seeks to quantify self-awareness. It wants to identify whether you are aware of your emotions and if you understand what is causing them. Since self-awareness is all about understanding your emotions and what influences them in order to be able to develop the self-management necessary to control them, this is an easy way to get straight to the point.

Just as the previous question scored answers, an answer of never warranted 0 points, rarely earned 1, sometimes earned 2 points, often earned 3 points, and always earned 4 points. Your answer of sometimes earned you 2 points toward your EQ.

Sample 3:

People often look to me to lead group projects at work or school.

1. *Never*
2. *Rarely*
3. *Sometimes*
4. *Often*
5. *Always*

Your answer here likely would have been 1. You never went out of your way to work with other people, nor did you ever try to assert yourself as a leader. You always did the bare minimum, and nobody in your workplace really trusted you since you never gave them a reason to do so.

This question sought to understand and quantify your relationship management skills. It wanted to identify whether you were often seen as a natural leader or if people naturally wanted to do as you said and follow your lead. Those with high relationship management skills are frequently seen as natural leaders in groups, and when they work in groups, people naturally want to do as the leader says because they do trust that person's judgment and know that he or she will do what is best for the team.

This question also uses the same scale of 4 points for always, 3 points for often, 2 points for sometimes, 1 point for rarely, and 0 for never. Your answer warranted a score of 0 in relationship management.

Sample 4:

I never concern myself with the welfare of others if it will be even a minor inconvenience to me to do so.

1. *Always*
2. *Often*
3. *Sometimes*
4. *Rarely*
5. *Never*

After reading this question, you circled that you agreed with the statement. If helping others took away from your time at work or any free time you may have earned by finishing your work quickly, you would disregard the possibility of helping other people. You did not see a reason to do so, especially if it meant extra work for you that you would not be paid for.

This question sought to quantify your social awareness skills. This particular question was concerned with empathy and how much you showed for other people. Those with higher social awareness skills act empathetically, wanting to help other people, even if it is somewhat of an inconvenience. They do not mind helping out, so long as it is not directly harmful to them, and sometimes even when it is. Empathetic individuals will act selflessly for no reason other than they feel as though they should do so because they can understand and feel the other person's pain or stress.

This question changed the scoring pattern. In this instance answering always warranted a score of 0 often would earn a score of 1, sometimes earned a score of 2, rarely got a score of 3, and never earned a score of 4. Your answer assigned you a score of 0 for social awareness.

Ultimately, after taking your four scores from the four questions, you scored 5/16 in emotional intelligence. This is quite low and requires work in all quadrants based on the four questions answered.

Chapter 5: Measuring Emotional Intelligence

Understanding that you can quantify your EQ is fantastic, but you need to understand more thoroughly how to judge what those scores mean. Why are certain scores important? How do they tell you what you need to know? Whenever you are testing something as abstract as emotional intelligence, it can be hard to really accurately quantify results. After all, the numbers used are going to be arbitrary based on whoever is executing the test. Some tests will have you answer out of 10 and provide you a score of 0-10 to decide how emotionally intelligent you are. Others will provide it out of 160. This book will have you ultimately calculate your score with a max of 40 points per quadrant, totaling 160 when your individual quadrants are added together.

How Emotional Intelligence Is Measured

As mentioned, your score will be measured out of 160 points. Each question you will answer in the next section can provide a minimum of 0 and a maximum of 4 points toward your quotient, just like in the sample questions that were discussed in the previous chapter. The questions that will be provided are carefully considered to analyze each of your four emotional intelligence domains. Each domain will involve 10 questions, providing a minimum score of 0 to a maximum score of 40. You will ultimately add up your scores after completing the questionnaire, and that is what you will use in order to identify what your EQ is.

When you have tallied up your score, you will want to compare it to the key that will be provided at the end. It will divide the possible scores into three different results that will tell you whether your score is low and requires attention to correct and develop it, effective, meaning that it is average, but could be strengthened, or enhanced, meaning you should utilize it to work on developing other quadrants that may be weaker or need work.

Remember, unless you somehow manage to score a perfect 160 on the test, there is always room for improvement. If you do not like the score you see in front of you after completing the assessment, you should use that displeasure as motivation to begin working on other aspects of yourself in order to better your emotional intelligence and strive toward a happier, more emotionally intelligent lifestyle.

At the end of the appraisal, you will be guided toward identifying your own personal weaknesses, as well as encouraged to work on the particular areas that are giving you a difficult time. You will learn where your weaknesses are through seeing your scores, and you will be given a baseline to work off of. Think of this first appraisal of your EQ as your pre-diet and workout weight and photos. This is where you are before you begin working to better yourself, and you should save it to look back on in the future after you have had time to dedicate toward growing your emotional intelligence. You may be surprised to see more growth than you initially expected, even after just a short time of working toward your goal of gaining a higher EQ.

How to Use Your Emotional Quotient to Understand Your Needs

Your EQ will be scaled into one of three categories: needing enrichment, proficient and functioning, or enhanced and strong. Understanding where each individual domain's EQ is will help you see where you are doing well and where you are struggling. If you know that you are struggling with self-awareness because you scored a 15/40, for example, you can use that knowledge to begin studying self-awareness. The last third of this book is dedicated to provide tips to improve emotional intelligence for each domain, and that is a fantastic first place to start improving yourself.

On the other hand, if you score 35/40 in self-awareness, but you have scored 12/40 in social awareness, you can use your skills in self-awareness to apply strengthening to social awareness. You already know plenty about your own emotions, needs, and how the world impacts them, so you can begin working to develop empathy skills instead. Your own self-awareness skills will be the foundation to bettering your social awareness.

When you learn where your domain skills fall, you are able to further understand your own behaviors as well. If you know that you have always struggled with managing your anger, for example, seeing that your self-management quotient score lowly may help you understand why and point you in the right direction to bettering yourself. You can meet that need to manage your own anger so it will no longer be overwhelming by following some of the practical tips toward bettering self-management. You will also be able to create concrete goals toward bettering your self-management and find guides to help you, step by step.

Ultimately, the most important way that knowing where your EQ sits on the scale is knowing your own weaknesses. One of the fundamental parts of emotional intelligence is having an understanding of your own weaknesses and developing them over time in order to compensate for that natural weakness. Because an EQ is not concrete or fixed, no matter which aspect is your weakest, you could theoretically work with it enough to make that weakness into your strongest domain. If you have always struggled with leadership but want to learn, that is a possibility, no matter what your temperament or current EQ. If your goal is to be highly emotionally intelligent with a strong relationship management quadrant, you can do that with the help of understanding where you are at now.

The Emotional Intelligence Scale

With many different methods to calculating emotional intelligence available throughout the world, it should come as no surprise that there are a multitude of scales available to judge that emotional intelligence as well. Each test is going to have a different scale that is used based on what is being measured.

The scale that this book will use is 40 points per quadrant with a max score of 160 for total EQ. Within this, scoring in the bottom 60% of any given category is seen as a weakness. Scoring between 60% and 85% is seen as being effective or proficient, but it could still be strengthened. Scoring in the top 15%, from 85% to 100% is seen as having enhanced or advanced levels of emotional intelligence. This higher level is incredibly tough to achieve naturally, but it can be consciously attained. See the following table for a basic breakdown of the results that will be used in this book's assessment.

Score	Individual Quadrant EQ	Combined EQ
Area for Enrichment: Needs work	0-24	0-96
Effective Functioning: Proficient, but could be strengthened	25-34	97-136
Enhanced: High EQ	35-40	137-160

Within this chart, you can identify the area for enrichment as a low EQ, effective function as average

EQ, and enhanced as high EQ. People within these different scores may behave vastly differently due to the many different possible combinations of EQ. It is entirely possible to have someone that excels at both self-awareness and self-management but is poor at social awareness and relationship management. That person's score could potentially report as effective, or average, depending on how they scored. For example, assume you scored a 35/40 on both self-awareness and self-management, but only 22/40 on social awareness and 18/40 in relationship management. This person's social skills are quite low and needing improvement while self-centered skills are enhanced. This person's total EQ comes out to 110/160, which puts him firmly in the center of effective, or average EQ, though he cannot navigate a social situation for his life. While his total EQ may be acceptable, he is going to struggle with those low social scores. Despite these sort of outliers, EQ is still a generally effective way to look at emotional and social skills.

With an idea of what the scale looks like, it is time to look at some of the most common traits of people with both low and high EQ.

Low EQ Traits

People with lower EQ typically are much more volatile and less stable than those with average or high EQ. They oftentimes are very emotional and unpredictable, and while they may come across as passionate and spontaneous to some people, it is actually a sign of lacking the emotional intelligence necessary to be successful socially.

- *Lacking control over their emotions:* People who struggle with their EQ frequently are controlled by their emotions rather than being in control. This can lead to situations that are emotionally charged quickly, becoming worse as fuel is thrown on the proverbial fire.
- *Does not understand the feelings of others:* Because those with lower EQs typically struggle with empathy, they frequently come across as clueless about other people's thoughts, feelings, or

needs, even if their feelings are clearly displayed on their expressions.

- *Lacking friendships, or failing to maintain them:* Those who struggle with EQ frequently also lack meaningful relationships with friends due to not having the emotional intelligence necessary to maintain those relationships. Due to the volatile tempers of those with lower EQ and a lack of good problem-solving and conflict resolution skills, friendships rarely last.

- *Keeps a straight face:* Those who keep their faces blank at all time typically struggle to express their own emotions. This is often due to a lack of understanding how to express their own emotions, a crucial component of emotional intelligence, rather than a need or desire to keep their emotions shielded away.

- *May be emotionally inappropriate at times:* Because people with lower EQ tend to struggle with reading other people's emotions, they may behave inappropriately, such as making a joke at a funeral or talking about sexually explicit topics at a family-friendly party with children present.

- *Cannot identify emotion from tone of voice:* People who struggle with EQ frequently struggle to identify emotion from voice alone. While people with average or higher EQ are able to identify the emotion being conveyed by tone alone, people with lower EQ typically fail to do so.

- *Lacks sympathetic behaviors:* Both empathy and sympathy require sophisticated emotional intelligence skills that those without much EQ typically lack. Because both empathy and sympathy require the emotional states of another person to be understood, it can be a big struggle for those with lower EQ.

- *Emotional reactions are typically intense:* Along the lines of being unable to control their emotions, those with lower EQs typically react incredibly strongly or intensely, even when it is not necessarily warranted. If something is annoying, they become irate, or if they are happy about something small happening, they may be absolutely ecstatic. These extremes are felt due to a lack of emotional control to keep reactions at an appropriate level.

- *Does not respond emotionally to movies:* Oftentimes, we feel emotional attachments to characters we see on TV. In a love scene, our feel-good hormones are pumping. In a tense horror scene, our own heartbeats quicken in response. These are empathetic responses with the characters in the movie or show, and someone lacking emotional intelligence is not likely to feel emotionally moved the same way as someone with a higher EQ.

- *Downplays the importance of emotions:* Almost as though they are in denial, oftentimes those who struggle with emotional intelligence typically try to downplay the importance of emotions and being able to communicate with them. They say that logic is more important, and lacking emotion is not nearly as much of an issue as lacking rationality. This is not true; however, as emotions and emotional intelligence are crucial to virtually every aspect of society.

- *Struggles with communication:* While the emotionally intelligent person is able to communicate tactfully, someone lacking a high EQ often resorts to name-calling, misdirection, and pushing the blame for situations onto the other person. This only serves to escalate the situation, rather than helping to deescalate it.

High EQ Traits

People with high EQ are typically much more adept at social situations than those with lower EQs. They are skilled at reading other people and juggling the needs of everyone, making sure that everybody is as satisfied as possible because of their own empathy. They are happiest when everyone else is content. These are some of the most common traits someone high on the EQ scale may exhibit:

- *Able to accurately name and describe a wide range of emotions:* Someone with high EQ is able to describe complex emotions beyond bad or good. They can say that they are feeling despondent or explain that they feel optimistically hopeful. Experts in the field have found that only about 1/3 of people are capable of this.
- *Balances rationality with emotionality:* Emotions do not run the show, though they may influence it.

People with high EQ are able to think rationally during emotional times, and they are able to use this skill to make good decisions, even during tough or distracting times or events.

- *Curious about others:* The curiosity of other people developed, regardless of whether you are actively interacting with that other person, is a byproduct of empathy. Because you are able to feel the emotional energy of other people, you become more curious about how others are doing.

- *Can regulate negative emotions:* While people with high EQ do not seek to avoid or quash any emotions they are feeling, they are able to regulate their reactions to them. Even when angry or scared, they are able to allow the rational part of their minds to control the situation. They never allow the negative emotions to overpower their rational thoughts.

- *Aware of strengths and weaknesses:* Because they are aware of themselves, they are able to recognize their strengths and weaknesses effectively and use that knowledge to prevent weaknesses from upsetting them or keeping them from succeeding. They are able to compensate for their weaknesses by using their strengths to their full advantage.

- *Good at judging other people's characters:* Because emotional intelligence is comprised mostly of social awareness, reading other people is a necessity. Those with high EQ have mastered this skill, and are able to make snap judgments about other people that are typically quite accurate.

- *Can manage toxic situations:* Because people with high EQs are able to control their own emotions and reactions, they are not fazed by the antics of toxic people. They are able to remain rational, which allows them to look at the situation empathetically to look for some sort of compromise that allows for the toxic situation to be deescalated.

- *Understand that perfection is unattainable:* People with high EQs know that perfection is impossible and do not seek it out. They understand that they will fail sometimes, and understand that they will have negative emotions related to failing. They do not feel as though failure has to be avoided at all costs because they recognize that everyone fails sometimes.

- *Take personal time:* People with high EQ are masters at managing their own emotions and stress levels. They frequently take personal time to allow them to do so.

- *Has power over negative thoughts:* While everyone is bound to feel negatively and have negative thoughts sometimes, those with high EQ are able to shut that negative narrative down. They look at the situation rationally, disconnecting their thoughts from their feelings through mindfulness in order to keep from spiraling into a cycle of negativity.

- *Can communicate and resolve conflicts skillfully and tactfully:* Those with high EQ are capable of looking at other people's perspectives, even in arguments, and use that skill to resolve conflicts without allowing resentment to fester in relationships. Their communication skills are much more tactful than those with lower EQ, designed to keep the other person's perspective in mind while still conveying the message.

- *Resilient:* Those with high EQ are capable of rolling with the punches. Even in times of stress, they are able to react in emotionally intelligent ways. Someone who is afraid may be able to overcome their fear to protect their family or to save the life of somebody in danger because, even when emotions are running high, they are able to think about things rationally and separate their rational thoughts from the emotions that they are feeling.

Remember, most people do not fall solely into one category or the other. It is entirely possible to see a mixture of these traits or behaviors, though they tend to trend one way or the other. Someone with generally high emotional intelligence may have some of the low EQ traits and vice versa. People with average EQ are typically somewhere between the two extremes listed above. They may be generally decent at communicating and solving conflicts but may become a victim of their emotions, which could make it difficult to see clearly or rationally. Someone could be great at reading and meeting other people's needs but struggles to meet their own, instead choosing to sacrifice himself to meet the needs of other people. Someone incredibly emotionally intelligent may be great at communication and empathy but never responds emotionally to movies.

When trying to decide where on the spectrum someone falls, remember that almost everyone will have some low and high EQ traits. Very few people fall solely into the high EQ categories, and if they do, it is because of years of effort to strengthen their skills.

Now that you have made it through this chapter, try to identify where you think you might fall on the spectrum. Which of the high and low EQ traits do you notice that you exhibit? Do you think that your EQ is generally high, low, or average? Try to do this before moving on to the next section. The next chapter will be an assessment of your EQ, and it can be quite telling to predict where you may fall and see where you actually do. It can help you identify disconnects in your thoughts and behaviors and help you identify how accurate your self-awareness actually is.

Chapter 6: Emotional Intelligence Self-Assessment

With your predictions for how you believe your own emotional intelligence levels will look, it is time to prepare to take the Emotional Intelligence Self-Assessment. You have learned all about emotional intelligence at this point and are ready to see where your own EQ stands so you can begin to work on strengthening it. You probably have a pretty good idea of your own strengths and weaknesses within the concept of emotional intelligence, but it is always helpful to see those strengths and weaknesses quantified in some sort of way to remove the abstractness from the concepts.

Instructions for this Assessment

Set aside some time where you can sit down uninterrupted for at least 20 minutes. You want to go somewhere relatively quiet and free of distractions. Turn off or mute any cell phones and make sure you are somewhere without television or music playing in order to actually focus on the questions given to you. Gather up a piece of paper or a word document on your computer and label it with numbers 1-10 for each category.

You will record your answer to each question as the number of the answer for future scoring. For example, if you choose answer 3. Sometimes as the answer to that particular question, you would record 3 on your scoresheet for future reference.

Remember, each question should be given proper consideration, and you should answer each question as honestly as possible. In order to ensure the most accuracy, you must consider each question and choose the answer that best suits you. You have a choice of 5 answers per question, and you should be able to identify one of them that works for you.

When you are answering questions, make sure you pay close attention to the order and scale of the answers. Sometimes, they ask for your agreement or disagreement, while other times, they ask how frequently you do something.

They sometimes flip with answer 1 being always some of the time while answer 1 can be never other times. You must answer the questions according to the scale provided in each individual question in order to ensure your results are accurate.

Now, without further ado, it is time to begin your assessment!

Self-Awareness

1. I frequently feel nervous or anxious about situations I am in, and I am frequently unsure why I am feeling the way I do.
    1. Always
    2. Often
    3. Sometimes
    4. Rarely
    5. Never

2. I typically try to avoid negative or troubling topics because they make me feel bad.
    1. Always
    2. Often
    3. Sometimes
    4. Rarely
    5. Never

3. My negative thoughts typically spiral out of control, and I struggle to reign them in. As soon as they start, they seem to have a mind of their own.

1. Always
2. Often
3. Sometimes
4. Rarely
5. Never

4. I am very stubborn or hard-headed and have a difficult time admitting to being wrong or taking fault.

1. Always
2. Often
3. Sometimes
4. Rarely
5. Never

5. I am able to motivate myself to complete difficult or unpleasant tasks, even if I do not want to do them.

1. Never
2. Rarely
3. Sometimes
4. Often
5. Always

6. I can be civil and polite to someone that I dislike if there is a situation that requires me to do so, such as at a business meeting or during a family event.
    1. Never
    2. Rarely
    3. Sometimes
    4. Often
    5. Always

7. I frequently hide my true emotions or feelings from others because ultimately, emotions are unimportant when trying to act in a rational manner.
    1. Always
    2. Often
    3. Sometimes
    4. Rarely
    5. Never

8. I am comfortable handling unexpected roadblocks that I encounter in life, such as a minor car accident, or being laid off from a job.

1. Never
2. Rarely
3. Sometimes
4. Often
5. Always

9. I am able to point out the good things in life that balance out the negative, even in bleak situations or times that are dark.
    1. Never
    2. Rarely
    3. Sometimes
    4. Often
    5. Always

10. I am able to identify my emotions and accurately label and convey those feelings with words in ways that other people can easily understand (for example, telling someone that you feel anxious and agitated instead of saying that you feel bad).
    1. Never
    2. Rarely
    3. Sometimes

4. Often

5. Always

Self-Management

1. I make sure I adjust my behavior to reflect who I am interacting with (for example, speaking professionally and politely with my coworkers while speaking much more casually and joking around with my friends).
   1. Never
   2. Rarely
   3. Sometimes
   4. Often
   5. Always

2. If I can tell that someone I am interacting with is feeling uncomfortable or intimated by me, I attempt to change my own behavior in order to make him/her feel more relaxed (for example, making a few jokes, lightening the tone, or adjusting body language).
   1. Never
   2. Rarely
   3. Sometimes
   4. Often

5. Always

3. When I am feeling anxious or afraid, I am able to calm myself down and regulate my feelings rather than falling victim to negative thoughts.
    1. Never
    2. Rarely
    3. Sometimes
    4. Often
    5. Always

4. I struggle to make decisions in periods of emotional turmoil and freeze up in emergencies or other tense situations.
    1. Always
    2. Often
    3. Sometimes
    4. Rarely
    5. Never

5. I know exactly what role I can play on a team and how my own strengths can be valuable assets, and I can convey that message clearly and efficiently.

1. Never
2. Rarely
3. Sometimes
4. Often
5. Always

6. I am always looking for ways to improve myself and strengthen my skills. Self-improvement is never finished, and there are always different ways to improve, even when you may not feel like it.
   1. Disagree completely
   2. Disagree somewhat
   3. Neither agree nor disagree
   4. Agree somewhat
   5. Agree completely

7. When I notice my emotions that I am feeling, I am able to accurately convey why I am feeling the way that I am, even if the cause of the emotion is somewhat obscure (for example, feeling sad on an anniversary of a bad event, or being reminded of grief because you saw something that reminded you of someone you lost).

1. Never
2. Rarely
3. Sometimes
4. Often
5. Always

8. I feel the need to consult other people before making emotional decisions.
   1. Always
   2. Often
   3. Sometimes
   4. Rarely
   5. Never

9. I struggle with expressing myself when things get emotional and tend to shut down as opposed to open up in times of need or in stressful situations.
   1. Always
   2. Often
   3. Sometimes
   4. Rarely
   5. Never

10. When I feel as though I am stressed out, and life is overwhelming, I feel as though I should give up.

    1. Agree completely

    2. Agree somewhat

    3. Neither agree nor disagree

    4. Disagree somewhat

    5. Disagree completely

Social Awareness

1. When arguing with someone, I typically seek to compromise in order to end the conflict without either of us feeling as though we are the loser.
   1. Never
   2. Rarely
   3. Somewhat
   4. Often
   5. Always

2. I find it difficult to take a look at someone else and understand how they are feeling by body language alone.
   1. Agree completely
   2. Agree somewhat
   3. Neither agree nor disagree
   4. Disagree somewhat
   5. Disagree completely

3. Listening to people discuss their opinions that differ from my own is upsetting for me, and I struggle to

see why they would think the way they do (For example, on topics surrounding politics or religion).

   1. Agree completely
   2. Agree somewhat
   3. Neither agree nor disagree
   4. Disagree somewhat
   5. Disagree completely

4. When discussing something with someone else who seems to have a more basic vocabulary, I often try to adjust my own speech without commenting on the other person's capabilities to match the other person's level for optimal communication. I want the other person to understand me, even if that means simplifying my own speech beyond what I normally would do.

   1. Disagree completely
   2. Disagree somewhat
   3. Neither agree nor disagree
   4. Agree somewhat
   5. Agree completely

5. I have no problems upselling someone a product that I know they do not need if it will better suit my own production or earn me a better commission, even though it will cost them money.

    1. Agree completely
    2. Agree somewhat
    3. Neither agree nor disagree
    4. Disagree somewhat
    5. Disagree completely

6. I am careful to word things in ways that I know are the least offensive in order to get my point across effectively and tactfully. I care about how other people are feeling and do not want to offend them.

    1. Never
    2. Rarely
    3. Somewhat
    4. Often
    5. Always

7. I am adept at handling toxic or high-conflict situations without letting emotions get the best of me. By making it a point to understand the toxic

person's position, I am often able to find an answer that does not leave one person walking away entirely dissatisfied.

    1. Disagree completely

    2. Disagree somewhat

    3. Neither agree nor disagree

    4. Agree somewhat

    5. Agree completely

8. I am frequently the voice of reason within my group of friends, and they frequently come to me during emotional periods for support.

    1. Never

    2. Rarely

    3. Somewhat

    4. Often

    5. Always

9. Seeing other people unhappy or hurt genuinely upsets me and motivates me to try to help them in any way that I can.

    1. Disagree completely

    2. Disagree somewhat

3. Neither agree nor disagree

4. Agree somewhat

5. Agree completely

10. I always consider how my own behaviors influence those around me when deciding the best course of action.

    1. Disagree completely

    2. Disagree somewhat

    3. Neither agree nor disagree

    4. Agree somewhat

    5. Agree completely

Relationship Management

1. I am able to motivate change in other people, both good and bad. People often look to me as inspiration and seek me out for advice on how to proceed in difficult or emotional situations because I have established myself as capable of being able to navigate through those difficult situations without allowing emotions to cloud my judgment.

    1. Disagree completely
    2. Disagree somewhat
    3. Neither agree nor disagree
    4. Agree somewhat
    5. Agree completely

2. I can handle emotionally stressful or volatile situations calmly and can function rationally during emergencies, even when feeling intense emotions at the same time.

    1. Disagree completely
    2. Disagree somewhat
    3. Neither agree nor disagree
    4. Agree somewhat

5. Agree completely

3. I naturally fall into leadership roles during group projects at work and school due to my ability to recognize and juggle all of the members' unique needs, strengths, and struggles while balancing them with the need to complete the project.
    1. Never
    2. Rarely
    3. Sometimes
    4. Often
    5. Always

4. I can recognize that sometimes, the best course of action is to change, and I am not afraid to be the person that triggers or initiates the change, especially if those around me are hesitant to do so.
    1. Never
    2. Rarely
    3. Sometimes
    4. Often
    5. Always

5. I can identify the strengths and weaknesses of people around me, as well as the ways that the other people can build upon their strengths and work to strengthening their weaknesses in order to better themselves, and I can tactfully provide the feedback and criticism necessary to inspire the betterment of those around me without offending them.
    1. Disagree completely
    2. Disagree somewhat
    3. Neither agree nor disagree
    4. Agree somewhat
    5. Agree completely

6. People often feel inspired to do what I want them to do and frequently agree to do whatever I ask of them because of the way I go about asking for it. I am generally described as influential and charismatic.
    1. Disagree completely
    2. Disagree somewhat
    3. Neither agree nor disagree
    4. Agree somewhat

5. Agree completely

7. I am considered trustworthy by most people I meet, and because of that trustworthiness, I am often able to foster a sense of teamwork within other people if I encourage it.
    1. Disagree completely
    2. Disagree somewhat
    3. Neither agree nor disagree
    4. Agree somewhat
    5. Agree completely

8. I can listen to a disagreement between two people and carefully consider both positions before explaining each view in a tactful manner that allows the other person to better understand the opposing viewpoint, enabling me to quickly and efficiently solve disagreements between other people and calm the situation.
    1. Disagree completely
    2. Disagree somewhat
    3. Neither agree nor disagree
    4. Agree somewhat

5. Agree completely

9. People often describe me as inspirational and say that my charisma and social skills frequently encourage those working with me to do their best work. My own eagerness to complete the task and create a positive workplace environment triggers others to want to do the same.
    1. Disagree completely
    2. Disagree somewhat
    3. Neither agree nor disagree
    4. Agree somewhat
    5. Agree completely

10. Because I am an excellent judge of character, I can typically identify people's strengths and weaknesses and use that information to create teams of people that work well together and bring out the best in each other.
    1. Disagree completely
    2. Disagree somewhat
    3. Neither agree nor disagree
    4. Agree somewhat

5. Agree completely

Calculating Your Scores

Congratulations! You have completed the questionnaire. That was the hardest part of this process. From here, your next step is to begin calculating your EQ, both in individual quadrants and as a whole.

The simplest way to do this is to add up the answers you got in each quadrant and subtract 10. The answers were designed, so every 1 was worth 0 points while every 5 was worth 4. The EQ score is calculated by taking the number of the answer you chose (let's say x for ease of understanding) and subtracting 1. So the equation on an individual level is x-1= total EQ points per question with x being the number of the answer you chose. You can calculate it out by doing that for each individual score and then adding it all up at the end, or you can shortcut by simply subtracting 10 from the entire sum.

This means that your quadrant score is calculated by adding up all of the answers within that quadrant and subtracting 10. When you have your four quadrant scores, you can add them together to get a total EQ score as well to get an idea of how well-rounded you are.

Remember to record both your quadrant and total EQs so you can begin to understand your score. Now that you have your scores recorded, it is time to begin interpreting each individual score!

Your Results

Remember the table provided for you in the previous chapter that told you what to expect in terms of the scale this test will use? It is time to refer to that again. For ease of access, the table will be repeated here. This is the same table that was shown before with no changes made. It shows you how your score should be interpreted. In any given individual quadrant, a score of less than 24 means that area needs work to bring it up to functional. A score above 35 means that that particular skill is quite developed and you should consider it a strength, with anything between 24 and 35 being effective. It does the job, but is not necessarily strong and has room for improvement.

Score	Individual Quadrant EQ	Combined EQ
Area for Enrichment: Needs work	0-24	0-96
Effective Functioning: Proficient, but could be strengthened	25-34	97-136
Enhanced: High EQ	35-40	137-160

With this table, identify which ranges your EQ falls into and see the following categories for understanding what this means for you.

Low EQ (0-24 individual quadrant or 0-96 total points)

With lower EQ, you often struggle with emotions and social situations in general. You are not in control of yourself or your life, and your emotions rule you. This frequently pushes other people away and makes understanding other people's communications with you quite difficult. You are easily offended and easily triggered into negative emotions.

You do not feel very good about yourself, and you may be very aware of how you never seem to quite mesh with people in social settings. You struggle with relationships of all kinds, and no matter how often you may try, you fail to better the relationships. You cannot help the urge to yell during arguments or disagreements, and because you cannot work through your emotions, people tend to avoid you.

You are ultimately likely incredibly unhappy in your life. You are frequently, or sometimes always, frustrated, feeling as though no one is understanding you without realizing that no one is understanding you because you are not communicating effectively. This only exacerbates your negative emotions as you are not only feeling upset or angry, but you are also further angered or upset because no one seems to understand the base feelings and you are unable to communicate them.

If you scored in this category, you have plenty of work to do to get yourself up to par emotionally. Scores in the low EQ range *require* further attention, or they will continue to be a detriment to you.

Average EQ (25-34 individual quadrant or 97-136 total points)

People with an average EQ are fully functional members of society. If you scored within an average range, you typically get along with others well enough, though there may be some conflicts here and there that can create bumps in your relationships. While you like yourself more than someone with low EQ, you still recognize that you sometimes struggle with your emotions. You are able to control them when they are not particularly strong, but when you begin to get overwhelmed, you may lose that control you have. You may hurt your relationships sometimes, but you are also able to recognize when you do so and work to repair them.

You are willing to take responsibility for your actions if they cause problems in other areas in your life, but it typically happens after you have had the time to cool down and recognize that you said or did something that you wish you may not have. You may struggle to let go of mistakes that you or others make, and you may hold grudges.

While you are able to navigate social relationships well enough, they are frequently bumpy, and you still find yourself struggling from time to time. You wish that you were better at your relationships and that you could change who you are. You wish that you were better at managing your own emotions, especially during times of stress when you *know* that those are the most important times to have control of your emotions. Despite knowing that, you struggle.

If you have scored in this category, you are emotionally intelligent enough to get by and not fail at every social situation you have, but you still feel the struggle of acknowledging and managing both your own and other people's emotions, and that struggle can lead to feelings of unease and unhappiness, while also contributing to feelings of anxiety and stress. You should consider strengthening the quadrants that scored within this range, building upon the skills you already have, in order to feel more secure and established. The better your emotional intelligence, the more secure and successful you will feel, and the more successful your relationships will be.

High EQ (35-40 individual quadrant or 137-160 total points)

Congratulations! You scored as having high EQ in one or several categories! This means that you are quite emotionally intelligent. You are in tune with your own emotions and understand how they influence yourself and those around you, and you have also developed the ability to control and regulate your emotions, so they do not dictate your actions. You are true to who you are and have a solid idea of your identity, values, and beliefs, and you will act in ways that line up with them.

While you are also aware of your own emotions, you are able to recognize the emotions in other people as well. You are skilled identifying the emotions and needs of those around you and are able to juggle both their and your emotions. You are likely extremely empathetic, enabling you to navigate through complex relationships while also influencing and managing other people's emotions and actions. You are likely a natural leader, charismatic and charming, and people frequently seek you out or choose to follow you.

You are enjoyable to be around in a wide range of emotional contexts, and people want to continue relationships with you. You are good at managing conflicts and defusing tense situations, which makes you effective in leadership roles. You are mature and willing to take jokes flung your way, even if they are deprecating.

You are likely flexible and go with the flow. It takes a lot to shake you or break your confidence, and most of the time, you are able to work with even the most difficult of unforeseen circumstances.

If you have scored highly in any of your emotional intelligence quadrants, you should use the skills you have in order to strengthen weaker quadrants in order to bring your total EQ up to this category. If all of your scores fall within this category, there is still work you can do to further develop and maintain your skills! Do not feel as though just entering this category is enough to warrant giving up on developing your skills. Seek to identify your weakest quadrant and start trying to bring it up to the same level as the highest.

What Now?

With your understanding of your scores, you are ready to move on to the next step: Strengthening your EQ! You now know what your strengths and weaknesses are, and with that in mind, you can focus on the relevant sections in the next part of this book. Part III will provide 50 practical tips for each realm of emotional intelligence to help you begin to better your own EQ.

Remember, no one is ever done working on their EQ. Even if you score highly, you can still learn from the tips provided in the next section of the book. Practical advice can teach you new ways you may not have considered before to practice and maintain your EQ. Even those with high EQ levels will begin to lose those skills if they do not maintain them, and even those with high EQ levels are not perfect. Everyone has weaknesses that they should strive to reinforce to better themselves.

Part III:
Practical Tips to Improve
Emotional Intelligence

Chapter 7: 50 Practical Tips to Improve Self-Awareness

1. **Take time to reflect on emotions:** Every day, you should sit down and reflect on how you felt during the day. Think about how you responded to various situations, and name the emotion that was felt during that response, with particular focus on negative emotions. For example, if you feel as though your spouse is holding you to unfair expectations, how do you respond? How do you respond when a friend confronts you on something that you did that hurt his feelings? You need to be able to identify how you react in the moment to eventually begin to build up self-management.

2. **Keep an emotions journal:** Every day, write down the strongest emotions you felt throughout the day and reflect upon them. What made you feel that way? What was happening when you felt the way you did? Do you see any patterns?

3. **Be observant about your own current emotions:** Always be aware of how you are feeling in the moment. If you are stressed, acknowledge that. If you are sad, acknowledge that as well. You need to get in the habit of checking in with yourself to see how you are feeling if you hope to recognize your emotions in a meaningful way.

4. **Ask others about how you act:** Sometimes, getting feedback from other people is crucial to understanding how you are portraying yourself. This can offer you valuable feedback about whether you are communicating your own emotions and needs effectively, or whether you need to continue working on conveying how you are feeling in the moment.

5. **Practice pausing before reacting:** It is easy to react in the moment when emotions run high. You need to get in the habit of pausing, taking a deep breath, and deciding on what you will say or do next. By giving yourself that moment, you can

identify when something you wanted to say would not be conducive to bettering the situation.

6. **Ask yourself why you feel the way you do in the moment:** A large part of self-awareness involves understanding your feelings, including why you are feeling the way you are. You must be able to stop and analyze your feelings, including identifying why you feel the way you do if you hope to be in control of your emotions when you move on to self-management.

7. **Ask yourself what you can learn from criticism:** Criticism can be tough to hear if you already have low self-esteem. If you are not very emotionally intelligent, you may struggle regulating your disappointment when someone voices their criticism of you, but asking yourself whether that criticism could be beneficial to you allows you to make that criticism constructive instead of destructive.

8. **Ask yourself what you can learn from failure:** Like criticism, understanding what you can learn from failure to avoid repeating it in the future is important. If you learn from your mistakes, you will grow, whereas if you simply avoid trying again, you have stunted yourself.

9. **Practice using more descriptive vocabulary about emotions in general:** When you feel sad, are you despondent? Disappointed? Ashamed? Fragile? Lonely? Learn to be more specific than sad, happy, angry, or other blanket emotions. This could be the perfect time to open up a thesaurus and widen your vocabulary.

10. **Always name every emotion to yourself as you feel the strong ones:** When you are feeling particularly emotional, make it a point to identify it. Putting a name to the emotion helps you understand what you are feeling, and also may help you regain control of the situation.

11. **Vocalize your emotions when talking to people you are close with and pay attention to how your voice changes based on your feelings:** People's voices change based on their emotions. You can hear the emotional crack in someone full of despair, or the harshness of the tongue when enraged. Listen to how your own voice changes when you are feeling a range of emotions.

12. **Practice pushing yourself out of your comfort zone:** No one likes being uncomfortable, but sometimes, you need to push yourself to get it over with. Just as sometimes, it is better to rip off the bandage, it can be better to force yourself into uncomfortable situations so you can learn to manage them. Be realistic with this step and slowly work yourself into uncomfortable situations as opposed to throwing yourself deep into your emotional triggers.

13. **Identify your emotional triggers:** Speaking of emotional triggers, learn to identify yours. You

need to understand the things that are most likely to set you off so you can be prepared when you notice one of your triggers nearby and begin to rein in your reactions.

14. Do not discourage or judge your feelings as they occur: Good or bad, and you should allow you to feel your entire range of emotions. Just because you acknowledge them and feel them does not mean that you are a slave to them.

15. Avoid making important decisions when in a bad mood: Making decisions in a bad mood can lead to impulsive choices that you regret later. Reserve decision making for when you are calm.

16. Avoid making important decisions in a good mood: Similar to making choices when in a bad mood, making them in a good mood can also sway you to take risks you would otherwise be uncomfortable with.

17. Check in with yourself during stressful situations and identify your emotions in that

moment: Especially when you notice that you are stressed out, you should check in with yourself. Identify how you feel in the moment and use that feedback to adjust your behaviors accordingly.

18. **Attempt to identify emotions of characters in the media:** Since a big part of being emotionally intelligent involves identifying emotions, try to practice identifying the emotions of other people as well. This is beginning to bridge your self-awareness skills to social awareness.

19. **Practice identifying expressions either online or with a trusted friend:** Make expressions related to various feelings and see if your friend can identify yours. This can give you an idea of whether you are communicating your emotions clearly or not.

20. **Pay attention to what happens in your body during emotional events:** When you are feeling high levels of emotion, pay attention to how your body feels and the body language you exhibit. If you are happy, are you smiling with a relaxed

body? If angry, are you tense with your fists clenched or your arms crossed?

21. **Recognize that negative emotions are important and useful:** Negative emotions should not be avoided. They need to be embraced and understood if you hope to be an emotionally intelligent individual. You must be able to read a wide range of emotions, including the negative ones. They serve their purposes just as much as the positive emotions and deserve that recognition.

22. **Look for patterns in your emotional reactions:** Similar to the act of identifying triggers, and you should also identify patterns in all forms of emotional reactions. Identify what makes you a certain way by making a mental or physical note of what preceded the emotional reaction. Eventually, you may begin seeing patterns in which feeling supported leads to you being happy and relaxed, or being busy tends to flare up your stress and anger responses.

23. Practice mindfulness: Mindfulness is the act of separating your actions from your emotions and allowing the emotions to occur while you observe them. Take a back seat and let your emotions free while you attempt to analyze them from a detached perspective. This may provide valuable insight to what is causing your reactions.

24. Stop treating your emotions as good or bad and start acknowledging them for what they are: Emotions all serve important purposes, and assigning them a normative value devalues them. You need to recognize that you are feeling your emotion for a reason, regardless of whether it is good or bad. You should not seek to avoid negative emotions, but rather to understand and utilize the negative emotions felt to respond appropriately to the situation.

25. Become comfortable in your discomfort: You need to learn to not shy away from your discomfort. As much as you may want to avoid it, learning to acknowledge and accept your discomfort is a surefire way to being able to control your own emotions. You must be okay with being in discomfort if you hope to be able to strengthen your self-motivation later on in the process of strengthening your emotional intelligence.

26. **Identify your values:** Understanding what you value is the first step in understanding what is motivating your behaviors. Take the time to acknowledge and identify the things you value most. This could be family, relationships, money, success, fame, reputation, or anything else.

27. **Identify how your values influence your behaviors:** Once you understand what your values are, take the time to notice how those values affect your behaviors. Do you act in ways that are conducive to your values? If not, how can you fix your behaviors to ensure that your values and behaviors line up? You will be much happier without that sort of cognitive dissonance in your life.

28. **Create life visions based around your values and decide where you would like to be in the next five years:** With your understanding of your behaviors and your values, identify where you would like to be in five years. This should line up with your values, so if what you value beyond everything else is family, it may be related to your own marital and parental status. If you value success, you may decide that you want to achieve a promotion or two during that period.

29. **Learn your stress cues:** What do you do when you are stressed? Do you withdraw or become aggressive and agitated? How do you respond physically to stress? Does it make you nauseous or leave you itching for a fight? Do you lash out or shut down?

30. **Observe how your emotions seem to spread through your entire body and the effects they have:** Emotions are contagious, and while they

may start in the mind, they quickly impact the rest of your body as well. Happiness may leave you relaxed and refreshed while anger leaves you feeling physically stressed.

31. **Constantly pay close attention to your own reactions and emotional states, even when they are primarily positive:** You need to learn to identify your emotions, both positive and negative and identify how they make your body feel. Pay attention to your breathing, heart rate, and body language and begin to label the physical reactions with the emotions felt.

32. **Create a regret letter:** Addressing this to yourself at a younger age, write down what you regret doing so far. Apologize to yourself for making the mistakes you feel are particularly pressing, such as skipping out on an opportunity to attend a school you really wanted to for a lackluster reason. This acknowledges your own failures without making excuses for them. You are able to

practice addressing your own shortcomings to yourself, which is a low-risk situation.

33. **The funeral test:** In this activity, you should sit down and write your own eulogy. You should answer questions about yourself, such as how you would like to be spoken of at your funeral, what you want to be remembered for, and how people will think of you when you are gone, compared to how you think people would currently answer. This allows you to see, more or less, where you are now compared to where you want to be and allows you to further understand where you may need to make changes in life to make up for past mistakes.

34. **Write your most important tasks down daily:** Start each day asking yourself what you must accomplish during the day to reach your long-term goals. If your long-term goal is to strengthen your ability to read your own emotions, perhaps you write down three activities you will do for the day to reach that goal. This helps you identify your values and goals while giving you a clear-cut list

that will guide your behaviors, even when your emotions may be trying to lead you astray.

35.**Practice apologizing:** No matter how painful you may find it, make it a point to apologize for any mistakes you have made, or if someone comes up to tell you that you did something to hurt them. Make your apologies meaningful as well: Identify what you did in the apology and promise to try to avoid doing it in the future. Even if you may not have felt like it was a big deal, you need to recognize how your own emotions or behaviors influenced other people.

36.**Practice grounding techniques when feeling stressed or overwhelmed:** Grounding techniques can help you stop and identify how you are feeling in that moment. It brings back your awareness of your current state and allows you to act wisely.

37.**Question assumptions:** If you find yourself reacting to assumptions you have made about other people or their behavior, ask yourself why you made the assumption in the first place and analyze its validity.

38. Trust your intuition: We make snap judgments for a reason. Trusting your intuition is different from responding emotionally. Trust your intuitive judgments without allowing your emotions to rule the situation.

39.Listen to your inner monologue: When learning to track your emotions, allow your inner monologue to go uninterrupted while paying special attention to your train of thought. It can provide valuable information about why you feel the way you do.

40.Tell yourself 'no': Teaching yourself to refuse some instant gratification can teach you to control your impulses. Make it a point to tell yourself no to at least five different small temptations a day, whether they are a beer; time wasted watching cat videos or other junk food.

41.Hold yourself accountable: Acknowledge when you make mistakes and make it a point to tell yourself what you can do differently next time to avoid repeating them.

42.Stop the excuses: If you have made a mistake, do not make any excuses. Similar to holding yourself accountable, you should make it a point to own your mistakes and do not try to minimize or downplay them in any way, no matter how badly you think it will reflect on you.

43. Stop gut reactions: When lacking self-awareness, you run on auto-pilot and allow emotions to rule, responding with gut reactions. You need to stop those gut reactions in the act, or preferably before they happen.

44. Avoid negative self-talk: Do not talk down to yourself. This can lead to stress and anxiety and should be avoided. There is enough negativity in the world without you adding more toward yourself.

45.Learn about body language and use it to fix your own: Use biology to your benefit and take poses that naturally encourage hormones and confidence, such as standing straight up. Learn to mimic people that can communicate charismatically and effectively, such as hand gestures.

46.Understand your personality type: Take a personality test and identify whether you are an introvert or extrovert. It will explain an awful lot about your behavior if you understand what kind of person you are.

47. Meditation: Practicing meditation teaches you to get better at relaxing your body and focusing on your breathing. You will also learn how to keep your mind on track when it begins to wander.

48. Identify strengths and weaknesses: Consider what your greatest strengths and weaknesses are. Understanding these will make you more self-aware and allow you to utilize them where they can be beneficial.

49. Acknowledge you are not perfect: By accepting and acknowledging that you are not perfect, you alleviate the fear of failing. Failure is inherently human, and when you acknowledge that, failing becomes infinitely less frightening.

50.**Monitor progress:** Track where you are before you start trying to strengthen your self-awareness. Look at your EQ score and compare it to where you are a month or even a year from starting. See how it has changed.

Chapter 8: 50 Practical Tips to Improve Self-Management

1. **Breathing practice:** In moments of stress or high emotions, remember to regulate your own breathing. Be aware of how your breathing changes when you are stressed or angry and make it a point to regulate your breathing to control your mood. After a few deep breaths, you may find yourself feeling calmer and more in control of the situation.

2. **Weighing emotion vs. rationality:** Consider the pros and cons of responding to a high-risk situation with emotion and rationality. Is it something that requires passion and emotion, such as deciding whether to propose to someone? Or is it a situation that requires logic, such as deciding how much house you can afford with your current income? By being able to step back and weigh the benefits of responding emotionally and rationally, you will

begin to see a clearer picture of the situation at hand.

3. **Make goals known to those around you:** By making your goals publically known, you force yourself to be accountable for those goals. People will have expectations that you will meet them, and may even help you in the process of achieving your goals, which also asking as deadlines loom closer. What better way to kick yourself in gear than to make your goal known to others, especially when it is a goal that directly affects them?

4. **Take a moment to count to 10 before responding:** When you are feeling emotional in a situation, take a few seconds to take in a deep breath and count to ten in your head. This allows the moment of emotion to pass and keeps you from reacting with negative emotions. You can instead respond with something that will benefit everyone.

5. **Take a night before you decide on important choices:** It can be easy to want to respond with

emotion when facing a big decision. Rather than making those decisions based on emotional gut reactions, give yourself a night to mull over the decision and allow the most intense emotions to pass.

6. **Talk to people who are skilled at self-management:** Get advice from people around you that are good at managing their own emotions. Those people may be able to provide you with their own tips and tricks to managing their emotions!

7. **Take the time to smile more:** Our bodies often respond with emotion to physical stimuli, and if you smile, you can improve your emotional outlook. Make it a point to smile and feel your entire emotional state begin to slowly shift to a positive one.

8. **Make time daily for problem-solving:** Schedule in a time that allows you to address the day's problems tactfully. This way, if you run into a complication during the day, you know there will

be time to address it later if it can wait, and it becomes less stressful.

9. **Control your inner monologue:** It is hard to be outwardly positive and in control of your negative emotions when they are running rampant in your mind. Make sure that you control your thoughts and keep them away from negativity. Use the skills developed in self-awareness, such as meditation, to keep your mind on track.

10. **Drown out negative thoughts with positive ones to keep yourself motivated:** Challenge yourself to come up with two positive thoughts every time you have a negative one. This drowns out the negativity and allows you to see positives that you may not have considered otherwise.

11. **Visualize what success looks like for you:** Create a picture in your mind that you are working toward. Decide exactly what you want it to look. This is what you will seek to create with yourself and provides motivation. You know what success

looks like and will be able to clearly identify your goal.

12. **Plan the steps necessary to achieve that success and act toward them:** Begin to plan out the steps that you will need to take to achieve your goal. If you want to be a more reliable friend, make it a point to plan out what a reliable friend will look like and what steps you need to take to make that happen, such as always following through with what you promise.

13. **Engage in self-care:** Make sure you maintain yourself. Take the time to exercise, eat healthily, and do something for yourself to alleviate stress levels. When your stress levels are lower, it is generally easier to control your negative reactions.

14. **Focus on your skills and abilities rather than on what you cannot do:** If you focus on the negative, your entire mindset will remain negative. Rather than dwelling on what you cannot do in a

situation, instead focus your attention on what you can do instead.

15.**Make it a point to take away something valuable from every encounter:** There is something valuable to learn within every single encounter, whether it is how your own body language or tone affected another person or how you responded in a certain situation. Make it a point to find something valuable in encounters, especially if you feel as though the encounter was pointless.

16.**Schedule in time for yourself to relax:** You need to keep your stress at a manageable level if you hope to be effective at managing your emotions.

17.**Recognize that you can strengthen these skills, and your current abilities are not your permanent limitations:** Your self-management skills are not inherent or fixed. Remind yourself that you can influence them, for better or for worse.

18. **Make a plan for handling your negative emotions when they occur:** If you struggle to react well in certain situations, try to make yourself contingency plans that will help you mitigate negative behaviors or thoughts. By having a plan, you will have something to fall back on if the stress is too much.

19. **Work on rewarding patience and discouraging instant gratification:** You want to avoid being impulsive or making decisions solely based on emotion. Try to reward yourself when you were patient and rational about a situation.

20. **Make it a point to control your emotions using body language:** Use your body language to influence your emotions. If you are keeping your body in a relaxed pose, your mind is more likely to follow through than if you are actively preparing for a fight.

21.Show people around you that you are listening and attentive with positive body language: Practice using your body language to convey that you are attentive to other people. You can communicate an awful lot just through facial expression.

22.Make plans to manage your stress levels: When stress begins to get to be overwhelming, create plans to bring it back to a manageable level. Perhaps you could break down whatever task you are working on into smaller steps, or take a break from the work altogether if that is an option.

23. Create a good work-life balance that is tolerable: You need an appropriate amount of time to yourself to enjoy with your friends and family, and if you want to keep your stress levels down, you will find a balance between the work you have to do and being there for your loved ones.

24.Eliminate toxicity and negativity wherever appropriate: Just because you can deal with the toxicity and negativity does not mean that it is not draining. Remove things that bring you nothing but negativity. Without the constant negativity, you may be blown away by how much easier it is to manage your emotions.

25. Imagine a wide variety of different circumstances and predict how you will react within each: This is similar to planning out how you will handle negative emotions, but with a twist. You are to play out how the variety of scenarios will go and predict your own reactions and results, as well as how changing your reactions may impact the results. This is more of a thought experiment than planning out your actions.

26. Break your routine to get yourself out of an emotional funk: If you feel as though you are stuck in an emotional rut, you can kick yourself out of it by changing your routine. By doing something new and unpredictable, your body does not have a natural, habitual response, and you will be able to do a sort of emotional reset.

27. Create a schedule that you adhere to While this may seem counterintuitive after the previous suggestion, remember that schedules keep things manageable. If you are juggling a lot, setting a schedule with strict times at which you rest, work, problem solve, take time to yourself, and fit in anything else you need to, you will be able to better manage your needs. Having needs met means your emotions are easier to control.

28. Remind yourself that you are in control of your actions: No one makes you do anything. Only you can choose to do what you are doing. Keep this in mind the next time you are slipping into negative actions.

29. Remind yourself that emotions are fleeting: Remind yourself that your emotion is temporary and fickle. They are impacted by everything, and just because you feel one way at that moment does not mean it is appropriate to act upon it.

30. Remind yourself that emotions are nothing more than your brain trying to process data: By reminding yourself that emotions are simply data and not actions or orders, you remove the control over yourself from them. You recognize that the emotions are only as powerful as you let them be.

31. Treat others fairly and with respect: Remember to treat those around you kindly and fairly. You should treat them the way you would like to be treated. Yes, the kindergarten golden rule still applies in adulthood, even for people you dislike.

32. Always keep your word in order to develop trust with other people: In order to establish yourself as trustworthy, make it a point to always follow through with what you say you will do. Not only is this an excellent exercise in self-control, it also sets the stage for social awareness and relationship management.

33.Always look for learning experiences, even in mistakes or mishaps: Even if you mess something up, seek to learn from the mistake. Understand what you did wrong and learn from that to ensure you do not repeat it in the future. Sometimes, the best way to learn is to fail and face the consequences.

34.Challenge yourself regularly: Do not allow yourself to fall into complacency and comfort. You should always be seeking to better yourself and hone your social skills, especially if you want to have good leadership or relationship skills.

35. Always ask yourself how the other people feel in various situations: Practicing empathy in real time can be particularly useful in helping you manage your own behaviors. If you can see that your behaviors are hurting other people, you are more likely to rein in those behaviors in order to avoid inflicting that pain.

36. Encourage adaptability or flexibility through spontaneity: While routine is important, you do not want to become too rigid. Sometimes, spontaneity is the perfect way to practice your flexibility skills. You can challenge a friend to come up with an entire day's worth of activities with no input from you to see how you respond to the surprises and lack of a plan.

37.Continue to work with self-awareness techniques: Do not forget your prior skills that you practiced in self-awareness just because you have begun focusing on self-management. Remember to continue practicing labeling your own emotions in real time, while also applying them with empathy and seeing how other people are responding to your emotions.

38.Recognize the separation between yourself and your emotions: Remember, just because you feel emotions does not mean that you *are* your emotions. You can feel angry, sad, or even foolish or weak, without defining yourself. Do not allow your emotions to define you. Instead see them for what they are: Your current emotional state and nothing more.

39. Pick your battles: Even when something is bothering you, only push the point or challenge it if you feel like it is worthwhile. Sometimes, it is not worth the trouble to correct something or be bothered by something someone said. Only pick battles that you feel strongly about.

40.Let the little things go: Along with picking your battles carefully, know when it is okay to let things go. Sometimes, you have to agree to disagree and walk away from an argument for everyone's sake, and that is okay. Knowing when it is that time is a fantastic example of self-management skills.

41. Choose how you want to respond to a situation and stick to it: Is this a situation in which you want to be defensive? Offensive to protect your beliefs? Should you be doubtful of your actions? Or is this a situation in which you need empathy or self-awareness? Choose which of the responses you need and try to stick to it.

42.Ask for feedback from others around you: After handling an emotionally volatile situation, try asking someone who was nearby, but not involved in the situation actively, how they felt it was handled, particularly in regards to your own feelings. Make sure that you are open to hearing the potential criticism that you will receive in return.

43.Ask yourself how you would feel toward someone else behaving the way you are: Take a moment to reverse the roles in your mind. How would you feel if the other person were treating you the way you are treating them? If you feel as though you would be comfortable with it, then you are probably handling the situation well, whereas if you would be bothered, you may want to correct some of your behaviors.

44. Practice communicating clearly in ways that are not offensive and are tactful: Even when you may feel tempted to say something that you know is rude, and even if you feel as though that rudeness might be justified, try to find better ways to convey your point that are not offensive. This shows self-restraint, which is important when you are trying to manage your emotions.

45. Celebrate your successes: While you have learned that you should make sure you treat failures and mistakes as learning experiences, you should also recognize successes as worthy of celebration.

46. Listen to what others are saying and do not interrupt: Especially in situations in which someone else is complaining to you, make it a point not to interrupt. Even if you feel as though the problem is that person's fault in the first place if accusing them of failing is going to worsen the situation, simply provide an attentive ear. Pay attention to the other person's cues before providing your own feedback, and if you will be calling them out, make sure it is done in a tactful manner.

47. Remember that positive attracts positive: Just as ruminating on negative thoughts can continue to spiral your mood down, your own positive thoughts can become infectious as well. If you are generally behaving positively, you own emotions will better the moods of yourself and those around you.

48.Choose productive actions: If you choose to behave productively, you will find yourself feeling positively in general. It may be easy to slip into old habits or to choose gratification over productivity, but remember, you will be happier and less stressed if you ensure that your work is done before your time that you use for yourself.

49. Seek advice from someone who is not currently emotionally invested in your situation: This allows you to see someone else's perspective on a problem that you may have tried to solve but found that your methods were not very effective. You also may get feedback you never considered, such as one of your actions coming across as inflammatory.

50. Remember that this is a process: Recognize that there is never an end to learning how to self-manage. No matter how good you are at it, you are never going to be perfect. There will always be room to improve.

Chapter 9: 50 Practical Tips to Improve Social Awareness

1. **Make it a point to learn the name of everyone you regularly interact with:** This small step means that you have taken the time to acknowledge other people and you are willing to show them that they are important. This shows them that you acknowledge their existence and recognize them as individuals.

2. **Be mindful of your body language as you go through your day:** By presenting yourself as open and relaxed, people around you will feel more at ease, especially if they have to come up to you to speak or interact for any reason.

3. **Understand the importance of timing when delivering unpleasant news:** Knowing when to mention problems is almost as important as knowing how to break bad news. If you time what

you are saying just right, you minimize the risk of upsetting the other person.

4. **Have icebreaker questions planned to break the awkward silence:** Have some sort of conversation topic you can use during those awkward silences that tend to happen at the most inopportune moments. The other person will likely appreciate having the silence filled, and you may even manage to make a friend with a new person.

5. **Be attentive during meetings or interviews:** Especially during meetings and interviews, you should be focused on the other people in your group. Make sure that you are always showing signs of attentiveness, such as making eye contact and nodding your head.

6. **Always prepare for social gatherings:** When you know, you will be at a social event, make sure you have a few basic conversation topics to fall back on and that you have considered the setting, mood, and type of event. You would not wear a suit

to a football game, and likewise, you should not go to a causal birthday party expecting to speak about the most recent problem at work.

7. **Be in the moment with people you interact with:** Really give people you are talking to your undivided attention. Show them that they are valued and important to you when you are speaking to them. This strengthens relationships and also encourages more empathy and understanding.

8. **Identify the feelings of people out and about, even if they are strangers:** Take a day to people walk and identify how people may be feeling based solely on their body language. You can tell a lot based on how someone is behaving and holding themselves, and this is an excellent exercise in practicing being able to read someone else.

9. **Practice how to listen effectively:** Make sure that you are really hearing the other person, rather than pretending to listen while really thinking about

other things or doing something else. Giving undivided attention to someone shows respect and acknowledgement.

10. **Understand and accept differences and diversity:** Welcome that some people have different opinions, and that is okay. Even if you and your coworker do not agree, recognize that diversity allows for broader opinions.

11. **Practice empathy:** Make it a point to understand how those around you are feeling. Really feel what they feel, relating to them on a more personal level and use that to strengthen relationships.

12. **Try to see the bigger picture in your interactions:** What is the context of your interaction? Why are you having the conversation that you are? Is this important or conducive to the atmosphere of the group? Consider all of this.

13. **Identify the mood in the social setting:** What is the general mood of the group at this moment?

Is it somber? Why? Is it more lighthearted? How are people behaving? These types of questions will help you develop a deeper understanding of those around you.

14. **Observe how your words impact other people and learn from the reactions of others:** This is important to understanding how to communicate. You should be able to tell at a glance how other people are understanding your words. If they seem to be shying away from your words or tone, it may be time to reconsider your methods.

15. **Ask follow-up questions to develop a deeper understanding of what the other person is saying:** When you are listening to another person, make sure you ask questions about what is being said to not only show that you are listening but also to develop a deeper understanding.

16. **Change your tone to match the setting or audience:** Some people require different tones. You should speak to children differently than your coworkers, and people at a party differently than

people grieving at a funeral. Knowing how to adjust your behavior based on situation shows that you understand emotional intelligence.

17.**Remind yourself that not everyone has the same experiences or worldview as you:** Just because you have a deeply held belief does not mean that other people share that belief. Other people may have had the opposite experience or may have developed different worldviews that directly contradict yours. Recognize that they have every right to their opinion in the same way that you do.

18.**Pay attention to small details and quirks of those around you:** If you notice that people have routines that they follow, you will be able to notice when they do not follow that routine, which can cue you to double check that everything is okay.

19.**Especially in workplaces, do not interrupt people:** When you are listening, do not cut other people off to change the subject or argue. Your job is to listen well until it is your turn to talk.

20.**Maintain gentle eye contact while talking with other people:** By maintaining eye contact, you are cuing the other person that you are actively listening, and by making sure that eye contact is gentle and friendly, you are conveying that you are not a threat.

21. **Always apologize when it is warranted, and even if you have unintentionally insulted someone:** Being able to put aside your pride and apologize to someone else shows that you value and respect the other person's opinion and feelings. Even if what you are apologizing was not intended to be hurtful, you are acknowledging the other person's feelings as valid.

22.**Keep your cell phone or computer off or closed during social interactions, barring actual emergencies:** When you are interacting with someone else, make it a point to give them undivided attention. Do not make them compete with your phone or your computer. You should ideally have both put away out of sight when interacting with other people.

23.Ask guiding questions: When you are trying to understand a dynamic, situation, or another person's emotional state, especially relating to a conflict, asking guiding questions can get you the information that has not been provided that you need to proceed. By guiding the conversation, you may be able to fix the conflict.

24.Repeat back what was said to you worded slightly differently to confirm you understand: Yet another skill related to good listening, by repeating back what you heard, you not only cue that you listened to the other person, but also that you understood them as well.

25.Do not take notes during meetings or interviews: Note-taking is important in college when there are vast amounts of information to absorb, but in meetings, you are expected to contribute. Instead of focusing on taking notes, you should focus on developing a working understanding of the material through interactions.

26. **Help people when they seem stressed or overwhelmed:** Going back to empathy, you should seek to help other people just because they are stressed out. By doing so, you help ensure their needs are met and strengthen your relationship with them.

27. **Take a genuine interest in other people:** Be interested in what the people around you are doing, even if it something you personally do not care for. While you may not enjoy writing, you can still be interested in your coworker working on a novel and cheer for her when it is completed.

28. **Take a genuine interest in the welfare of the people around you and be willing to intervene if you can help:** Related to the prior step, taking an interest in the welfare of others can build

rapport with other people. People are more inclined to like you and trust you if you help them.

29. **Do not be afraid to suggest something new in a situation that is not working:** Social awareness involves being aware of how you can influence others, and that sometimes includes triggering change. Suggest a new perspective when you have a situation that is failing. It might be a perspective that has gone unconsidered until the.

30. **Always put the needs of the group ahead of the needs of yourself:** Because social awareness involves empathy and taking care of the group, there is no room for selfishness. You need to put the group ahead of yourself sometimes for the betterment of the entire group, and you need to know when to do that.

31. **Be honest in how you respond when asked, even if the honest response may be unwanted:** When someone asks you for feedback, you need to ensure that you provide it honestly and

thoughtfully. Even though sometimes, you may have to share an unpopular opinion, you should be free to share your thoughts.

32. **Communicate with tactful language:** By keeping your language tactful and neutral, you will be able to explain difficult or unwanted topics in a way that minimizes hurt or emotional harm. This is what doctors call bedside manner, and it is helpful in far more situations than just medical settings.

33. **Acknowledge the skills of other people:** Being able to look at other people and recognize their own skills and strengths takes empathy and social awareness. By acknowledging the other person's skills, you may be able to find ways that those skills can benefit everyone.

34. **Provide other people feedback to help them develop who they are:** Being able to see people's weaknesses is also important, as is being able to point out ways that those weaknesses could be

patched up to keep them from becoming too detrimental in the future.

35.**Limit or eliminate social media for a week or two:** We often spend far too much time obsessing over our social media, and it comes at a cost of empathy and isolation. By forcing yourself to step back, you will further foster actual human interaction instead of staring at a screen.

36.**Begin networking and meeting new people:** One of the easiest ways of developing social awareness is to go out and meet new people from all sorts of backgrounds. Meet people with new or different worldviews or people who are in different professions. You never know when you might meet someone who can help you in the future.

37.**Avoid voicing complaints:** If you want to bolster your social awareness, you need to avoid voicing too many complaints. Those complaints can bring the general atmosphere of the social interaction down as well as paint yourself as a victim that cannot fix the situation you are complaining about.

38. **Avoid causing drama, or allowing other people to cause you drama:** Along with avoiding complaints, you should seek to avoid drama. People, by and large, do not enjoy dealing with drama, and they will go out of their way to avoid it. Likewise, you should not allow other people the ability to influence you so strongly that they create drama for you.

39. **Try to keep your speech and general demeanor positive:** Positivity is infectious, and if you are able to keep your own speech and demeanor positive, you will see the positivity of the entire social setting increase.

40. **Avoid giving in to peer pressure, especially if whatever others are pressuring you into is something you do not agree with:** When you are in social settings, you may feel pressure to do things that you are not comfortable with. You

should not feel as though you have to sacrifice your own values for other people, especially if you disagree with them.

41. **Toe the line between helpful and overly critical:** It is important to be able to provide constructive criticism, but that criticism can quickly become negative and overbearing if you are not careful. You must be mindful to keep your criticism helpful without sugar coating it while making sure that what you are saying is still constructive.

42. **Do not dwell on the past, especially regarding what other people may have done to you:** Being able to recognize that the past is in the past and forgive others for mistakes, especially when those mistakes where truly mistakes and not intentional, you are recognizing the humanity in other people. You are recognizing and accepting that people are not perfect and sometimes make mistakes. This keeps you out of the negative grudge trap.

43.Join social groups with people who share similar interests as you: Further extrapolating on the importance of social interaction in order to develop social awareness, try to find groups outside of your comfort zone who share similar interests. You may be pleasantly surprised at the new kinds of people you can meet by joining clubs or groups in your area, and your social skills will thank you for it.

44.Compromise when there are conflicts: Recognize that there is no way for everyone to walk away from a conflict entirely happy. The best you can do is offer up compromises where each person gets some of what they need. Identifying conflicts and the compromises that can solve the conflict requires higher levels of emotional intelligence.

45.Find some sort of common ground between yourself and the other person: When you find yourself interacting with someone who seems entirely foreign to you, seeking out some sort of common ground is the perfect way to relate to each other. This can be anything from a common hobby or taste in music, or even as simple as having a sibling that is the same age. By connecting to someone when you first feel that connection is impossible, you are using your social awareness.

46. Pay attention to how closely people orient themselves to other people: Be aware of the physical distances between people. Those who are uncomfortable with one another typically keep a larger physical distance between them than people who are comfortable. This can be an important part of body language.

47.Volunteer and get involved in your community: This suggestion sees you getting involved in your community while also helping meet needs that would otherwise go unmet. This is the perfect way to practice your empathy and skills involving understanding diversity.

48.Observe how people naturally respond to you and respond to those reactions: You can tailor your own body language and communication skills to situations by watching how other people seem to react to you. This empathy makes you appear to be very emotionally intelligent.

49. **Use mindfulness to look past emotions and get a better understanding of the situations at hand:** When you are in an emotionally charged situation, remembering to step back with mindfulness to reevaluate the situation can help you see where a disconnect may be. Perhaps something you have said is insensitive. Knowing where you went wrong will enable you to correct for it.

50. **Continue to practice self-awareness and self-management to better your social awareness:** Remember, all of your emotional intelligence skills build upon each other. You need to maintain all of them to be a well-rounded individual.

Chapter 10: 50 Practical Tips to Improve Relationship Management

1. **Be open-minded:** You should be willing to consider anything anyone suggests to you without feeling strong emotions either way toward the suggestion. By being open-minded, people will not feel judged when they come to you with problems, suggestions, or other conversation topics. They will feel as though they can trust you, and that trust will go a long way.

2. **Enhance and deepen your communication:** Find your way of communicating and enhance it to make it as effective as possible. If you know that you like to make compliment sandwiches to deliver criticism, for example, master the art of tactfully explaining parts that need work.

3. **Communicate clearly:** Always be as clear as possible when communicating. Seek to use specific

language that is difficult to mix up or misunderstand. Words that lack ambiguity will be your best friend when trying to communicate clearly and effectively.

4. **Ask if others have any questions for you:** Always encourage those you are working with to ask questions after you finish explaining something. This enables them to mull over the material you have provided while also showing that you value them and their understanding.

5. **Remember to pay attention to details:** Small details in relationships and communication matter! Recognize even the smallest and most insignificant of strengths and weaknesses, as you never know when they will be relevant to your projects.

6. **Be welcoming to feedback:** Always welcome criticism, no matter how harsh, and make sure those you work closely with understand this. When you are provided with feedback, make sure you thank the other person for it and make it clear that

you mean it. If you are gracious about receiving feedback, even when it is negative, you are more likely to get honest feedback in the future.

7. **Be trusted:** Do everything you can to establish yourself as a trustworthy individual within your social and workplace groups. By being trustworthy, people are more likely to be swayed by your words because you have never steered them wrong before.

8. **Be the person anyone can talk to about anything:** An open door policy harbors further trust and makes people feel as though they can approach you without fear of judgment.

9. **Don't try to avoid what will happen anyway:** If the inevitable is something you would rather not deal with, it is better to get it over with quickly. This shows your social circles that you are not afraid to approach uncomfortable or undesirable situations quickly and with tact.

10. **Acknowledge the feelings of those within your groups:** This leaves all members of your group feeling validated, which in turn lends itself to creating a group of people more inclined to help you or follow your lead.

11. **Be a complementary person:** Always seek to insert yourself into situations that you know your own skills complement. If you are good at organization while another person is good at research, the two of you have skills that complement each other, and you could be valuable assets to each other.

12. **Be a complimentary person:** Yes, this is different from #11! Compliment people on a job well done. This acknowledgment of their skills and success will make those around you feel recognized and valued.

13. **Show that you care:** Little tokens of appreciation, such as a hand-written thank you note or a birthday card, let those around you know

that you value them as individuals and strengthens your relationship with them.

14. **Be decisive:** Do not be afraid to make a decision, especially when others seem to be struggling with the task of doing so.

15. **Explain why you make decisions:** Along with being willing to make the decision, you should have the tact and communication skills to explain to those around you why you made the decision you did.

16. **Be able to provide direct, constructive feedback:** You should be able to quickly and tactfully identify and suggest areas that those around you need to improve, with those suggestions developed after time spent getting to know the individual.

17. **Make sure your intention and impact are in sync:** Saying the wrong thing with the right intentions is just as harmful as saying the wrong

thing with the wrong intentions. Make sure that when you are wording something, especially if it is negative or a criticism, that you word it in a way that is constructive and cannot be misconstrued negatively.

18. **When addressing a challenge, offer a solution to it:** The solution should be something that you see as a potential fix to the problem! This points the other person in the right direction.

19. **Be able to handle tough or uncomfortable conversations with tact:** Do not shy away from difficult subjects. People will appreciate you more if you discuss things tactfully and directly.

20. **Set boundaries:** You should develop your own boundaries and enforce them. This lets other people know just how far they can go with certain things before you have a problem.

21. **Respect boundaries other people set:** Complementary to your own boundaries, you

should try to recognize the boundaries that other people set and enforce.

22.**Assume people mean the best, even when things don't work out:** Try not to be offended if someone struggles to communicate and bungles the message. Instead, assume they meant the best and move on with life. There's no use to clinging to negativity.

23.**Volunteer for uncomfortable leadership roles:** There is no better way to start practicing your relationship management skills than taking a leadership role. Even if you feel out of your element, give it a shot.

24.**Be willing to question status quo:** Do not be afraid to challenge how things are being done and suggest new ways to try things out.

25.**Offer advice and opportunities to help other people grow:** Whenever you are working with other people, offer ways that they could further enhance their skills, or even suggest that they try something new.

26. **Earn the loyalty of other people through your own actions:** Those with high relationship management quotas win the backing of people through their behaviors. You should make it clear that you are worthy of that loyalty by always seeking to help other people.

27. **Prove yourself trustworthy:** Always follow through with what you say you will do so people around you know they can count on you to help them when they need it.

28. **Be able to identify ways that other people can work together:** Especially if you are a leader in a group, try to pair up people who seem to work well with each other, whose skills balance out the weaknesses of the other person and vice versa.

29. **Learn to to quickly identify and deescalate conflict within groups:** Try to watch for rising

tensions so you can deescalate them before they blow up. This will further earn trust as you manage to stop conflicts in their tracks

30. **Give every member of your group a task that allows each to be productive in their own ways:** Being able to identify the different strengths people bring to the table celebrates diversity and develops trust that you are seeing a bigger picture.

31. **Be able to talk someone down from high emotions quickly and efficiently:** Learning this skill means that you have mastered the art of influencing other people's emotions. Other people may feel like you always have the right words for every situation.

32. **Develop the ability to relate to other people easily:** If you can relate to anyone quickly and easily, you are able to better empathize with them quickly, and they will be more inclined to listen to an empathetic person.

33.Be grateful when someone shows an act of kindness toward you: You should always show that you appreciate those around you, especially if they show an act of kindness. Send them a note thanking them or tell them in person.

34.Ask yourself what you can do for the people you believe can help you too: Before asking yourself what other people can do for you, you should first ask how you can benefit each other. Relationships should be mutually beneficial.

35.Always ask for what you want: The worst that can happen is someone says no. By always asking for what you want, you are clearly stating your desires, and those who agree or align their desires with you will be able to do so.

36.Always try to create win-win situations: Situations should create the best possible solution for as many people as possible. A situation in which one person is on top while everyone else suffers is not conducive to a team environment and should be avoided.

37. **Find ways to create a team identity:** Your team should be more concerned with a group identity and success than individual success. If you want to have higher relationship management skills, you should foster this through team-building exercises and rewarding them for group successes.

38. **Foster bonds within the team:** Along with a team identity, creating bonds within the teams encourages people to work with each other and genuinely enjoy doing so rather than seeing each other as inconveniences.

39. **Always show up a few minutes early:** To be on time is to be late, and is incredibly disrespectful. Instead, you should always aim to be at least 5 minutes early. This shows that you value the other person's time.

40. **Treat everyone you meet, no matter what they look like or how they act, as incredibly important:** Basic human decency says we all deserve the same basic consideration, and you should remember to acknowledge this.

41. **Under-promise so you can over-deliver:** This is a sort of work-around to managing expectations. If you promise to have something done by Friday to give yourself extra time, you can return the project by Tuesday and win brownie points for having it done three days early.

42. **Work with your peers' strengths and weaknesses:** When working with others, make sure you insert yourself in areas that you believe you will be the most effective and useful at complementing everyone else. This shows them that you are seriously considering their abilities and recognizing them on individual levels.

43. **Accommodate other people whenever you can:** Empathy allows for compassion, and by accommodating others, you are showing that you

are empathetic to the struggles of juggling both workplace and outer stressors.

44. **Understand that those you work with have lives outside of the office and that those lives should be the workers' priorities:** This may be one of the most important keys to remember to strengthen relationship management: Ultimately, people's loyalty will default to their families first and foremost, and if you can remember that, you will quickly become a close 2nd in their list of loyalty.

45. **Inspire others to try to succeed, even when the odds are stacked against them:** Be the reason that people try things that they will most likely fail. Encourage them to try and inspire them by trying to achieve the nearly impossible yourself as well.

46. **Seek to persuade other people without manipulation:** Learn how to ask and receive what you want or need without having to rely on

manipulation to get it. If you develop a good enough rapport with those around you, this should be a no-brainer.

47. **Create a productive work environment for yourself and others:** You want to make an environment that people are happy to enter. Happy people are more productive and more loyal people who will be more willing to try to help you if you ask for it.

48. **Always opt for personal interaction as opposed to digital when it is realistic and convenient:** To truly strengthen the bond between yourself and those around you, you should aim to make your communication as personal as possible. If you can do it face-to-face, that is preferred to digital or texting.

49. **Lead by being actively involved in the work rather than by dictating what other people do:** The easiest way to inspire others is to be involved yourself. If they see you in the trenches,

they see a leader who is not afraid to help them and get dirty, who is far more trustworthy than a leader who would rather sit back and order people around.

50. **Remember to use your self-awareness, self-management, and social awareness skills in all of your interactions!** As mentioned before, remember that all of your other emotional intelligence skills should be used toward strengthening your relationship management! Do not forget to utilize the most important skills within those quadrants.

Conclusion

Congratulations! You have made it through *Emotional Intelligence Practical Guide*! Hopefully, the information contained in these pages has been beneficial to your understanding of how emotional intelligence works, as well as toward your own current EQ. Throughout this book, you were provided with the knowledge you would need to begin taking control of your EQ and becoming a more emotionally intelligent individual, something that could have lifelong positive benefits to you.

As you make your way through your journey to higher emotional intelligence, be sure to remember some of the key features: You must understand how the four domains of emotional intelligence play off of each other and how each domain is important for social interaction. If you want to be a well-rounded individual, capable of empathy and emotional intelligence, you must have a fundamental understanding and control of your own emotions, as well as the empathy necessary to see how your actions and emotions impact other people. Without that fundamental understanding, your empathy will be meaningless, as you will be unable to relate to those around you.

Remember, you are not trapped at your current emotional intelligence level. Your EQ can grow or shrink based on your own personal behaviors, choices, and development. You can become as charismatic as some of the greatest leaders if you care to put in the effort, or you can retreat as much as you would like and avoid interacting with others. Ultimately, the choice is yours, but research has found that those with higher emotional intelligence levels tend to be happier and healthier.

If you do decide to move forward with bettering your EQ, do not forget the tips provided within these pages! Each tip and challenge requires you to work toward bettering each EQ domain, and if you are able to accomplish all of the challenges and suggestions, you will find your social skills increasing immensely.

Now that you have reached the end of this practical guide, it is time for you to begin! Go out and put your newfound skills to good use in the real world and see where they will take you! Work on strengthening your emotional weaknesses while relying on your strengths that were identified during the assessment. With your newfound knowledge, you are armed with what you will need to begin the process. Good luck, and please feel free to come back to this book as much as is necessary or beneficial to you!

Made in the USA
Monee, IL
30 October 2019

16071639R00127